SAMUEL BECKETT

Richard N. Coe

GROVE PRESS, INC.
NEW YORK

EVERGREEN PILOT BOOKS

Marillis
Marie
Meyers
1966

Chief Editor
A. Norman Jeffares

Advisory Editors
David Daiches   C. P. Snow

SAMUEL BECKETT

CONTENTS

ACKNOWLEDGMENTS

For permission to quote from the works of Samuel Beckett, acknowledgments are due to John Calder, Ltd., Chatto & Windus Ltd., Faber & Faber, Ltd., and Editions Minuit.

The photograph on the front cover is reproduced by permission of Michael Peto.

R.N.C.

ABBREVIATED TITLES
BY WHICH THE WORKS OF
SAMUEL BECKETT
ARE QUOTED IN REFERENCES

C.C.	=	*Comment C'est.*
E.	=	*Endgame.*
H.D.	=	*Happy Days.*
K.L.T.	=	*Krapp's Last Tape.*
M.D.	=	*Malone Dies.*
M.P.T.K.	=	*More Pricks than Kicks.*
N.T.P.R.	=	*Nouvelles et Textes pour Rien.*
T.N.	=	*Three Novels.*
W.	=	*Watt.*
W.F.G.	=	*Waiting for Godot.*

CHAPTER I

THE ART OF FAILURE

"Given the existence as uttered forth in the public works of Puncher and Wattmann of a personal God quaquaquaqua with white beard quaquaquaqua outside time without extension...." Lucky's celebrated "think" in *Waiting for Godot* is an extraordinary *résumé*—in a form which is by no means as garbled as might at first appear —of the Beckettian universe. Poor Lucky's initial premiss leads him nowhere. It is the ever-present, pathetic might-have-been of Beckett's thought. Before long, this strange "pensum" resolves itself into a lament—a lament for "man in short for man in brief," who everlastingly "wastes and pines," and whose inexplicable existence seems "for reasons unknown to shrink and dwindle" towards "the great cold the great dark the air and the earth abode of stones in the great cold alas alas ... the stones ... so calm ... Cunard ... unfinished."[1] Lucky's neurasthenic rationalism tails off into an incoherent Jeremiad of hopelessness; but to class Beckett himself as the simple incarnation of "despair" is a drastic over-simplification. To begin with, the concept of "despair" implies the existence of a related concept "hope," and "hope" implies a certain predictable continuity in time—which continuity Beckett would seriously question. "Despair," with all its inherent moral overtones, is a term which is wholly inadequate to describe Beckett's attitude towards the human condition; nor is this condition, in the most current sense of the definition, "absurd." It is literally and logically *impossible*. And in this central concept of "impossibility," his thought has most of its origins—as does also his art.

Unlike many of his contemporaries, Beckett has written very little, directly, about himself, still less about his aims and ideals as a writer. The Beckettian legend is one of silence. When Alan Schneider asked him who or what was meant by "Godot," he replied succinctly "If I knew, I would have said so in the play," and left it at that. In 1949, however, for the first and last time he broke this silence, and published in Eugène Jolas' perennially *avant-garde* review, *Transition*, a series of three "Dialogues" with the French art-critic Georges Duthuit.[2] Each of these brief, almost telegraphic arguments deals with a modern painter: the first with Tal Coat, the second with Masson, and the last—a most typically Beckettian piece of irrational dialectic—with Bram van Velde, an artist whose work has fascinated Beckett for more than twenty years. In these "Dialogues," although the subject is the abstract art of the nineteen-forties, Beckett reveals his own inner and formal preoccupations more clearly than anywhere else. Pure abstraction, argues Duthuit (or "D"), is "a liberation." The painting and the painter grow together, each is inherent in the other, and the final product, the work of art, is freed from the arbitrary tyranny of the objective accident, the "landscape seen at a certain age, a certain season, a certain hour." But Beckett (or "B") is not so easily won over. What is "abstraction," he retorts, if not the ultimate degree of naturalism, or "realism," in the sense in which Ionesco, for instance, would argue that *he* is a realist: a realism which includes the unseen as well as the seen, the dream in addition to the waking vision, the artist as well as the canvas? "Total object, with missing parts," he argues, "instead of partial object. Question of degree." Traditionally, the artist desires to "express" the object, the mood or the occasion of his vision; to express it the more fully in order to "possess" it, to petrify an instant of awareness into eternal immobility, to transmute it into a Thing: *his* vision, *his* landscape, *his* dream, now durable and portable, a piece of property. "Art has always been bourgeois."

But the "bourgeois" world was the reflexion of a certain order of beliefs and values, and these values Beckett no longer accepts. In the context of infinity, time and space themselves, let alone man, his visions and his property, are meaningless; and it is precisely this new awareness of the infinite—once comfortably inconceivable —that mathematicians and scientists have now deposited, as it were, upon our very doorstep. Around us on every side, in space, lies the Void; behind us, before us, in time, lies the Void; and when the universal ultimate is "das Nichts," then all normal concepts of significance become absurd. In such a context, "art" is irrelevant, impossible . . . unless there were to be discovered an art which could (literally) "express nothing."

Then what about Masson? In Masson, argues "D", there *is* a painter whose aim is—as far as may be—to "paint the void . . . in fear and trembling." But "B" is still not satisfied. To *want* to paint the Void still argues that the painter is held in the trammels of the old idealism. The Buddhist cannot desire Nirvana, because Nirvana, by definition, is that which cannot be desired. "Two old maladies . . .: the malady of wanting to know what to do, and the malady of wanting to be able to do it." The artist who "desires to express" the Void has in reality no concept of what the Void is (we shall see The Unnamable struggling with the same problem). The Void is not simply negative; it is not "the obliteration of an unbearable presence," nor is it defined by simply being indefinable; the "impossibility of statement" and the "anguish of helplessness" are assertions about the mentality of the artist—they tell us nothing about the Void as such. No statement tells us anything about the Void.

So little does "D" seem to appreciate "B" 's arguments that he concludes the Masson "Dialogue" with the affirmation that the function of art is to immortalise "the things and creatures of spring . . . in order that what is tolerable and radiant in the world may continue." At which point "B" "exits weeping." In the concluding "Dialogue," however, "B" himself brings forward, in illustration of his thesis, the Dutch painter Bram van Velde. Bram van Velde, a master of disintegrated forms arbitrarily held together in composition by an equally arbitrary girder-work of lines, has evolved a nihilistic style in which any image remotely suggested at one instant is brutally cancelled out and denied existence in the next. The resulting impression is very much that of a "void," not expressed, but violently and actively created by the act of painting. This, however, is not the Bram van Velde of Beckett's vision. Rather his situation is that

of him who is helpless, cannot act, in the event cannot paint, since he is obliged to paint. The act is of him who, helpless, unable to act, acts, in the event paints, since he is obliged to paint.

D: Why is he obliged to paint?

B: I don't know,

D: Why is he helpless to paint?

B: Because there is nothing to paint and nothing to paint with.[3]

Art, in fact, is the elucidation of the impossible. The human condition is that of an indefinable *Néant* within, conscious of a possible relationship with an equally indefinable *Néant* without, yet invalidating that relationship by the very fact of its consciousness. The artist is driven—by the very fact of being an artist—to realise, to create in art, that which is not, which cannot be, because, as soon as it is realised in concrete terms (paint or words) it ceases to be itself. Consequently, it *must* fail. Beckett's own art likewise is an art of failure: it is by definition trying to do something that it cannot conceivably do— to create and to define that which, created and defined, ceases to be what it must be if it is to reveal the truth of the human situation: Man as a Nothing in relation to all things which themselves are Nothing. "To be an artist is to fail," concludes "B" in the "Three Dialogues," "as no other dare fail. Failure is his world." And the same theme is echoed and developed by most of Beckett's people, in particular by the narrator of the *Textes pour rien*:

> "No, but one last memory, it may help, help to fail yet again."[4]

The gradual elaboration and application of this strange and quasi-mystical ideal of art and "reality" will be the main theme of this study. In terms of a different symbolism altogether, the condition of man is a kind of Purgatory, but of a very much more complex nature than that imagined by Dante. Man has a vision of Paradise—the ultimate realisation of the Self in a *Néant* beyond space and time, void united with void; yet to desire such a Paradise is to be aware of a Self desiring, and a Self desiring is not a void, and therefore cannot enter. The existence of man, then, is not Paradise; but neither is it Hell, for a sort of hope remains, the hope, not of achieving the impossible, but perhaps of discovering, in the very act of grappling with impossibilities, some new synthesis of the Self, detached from time and space and above all from language, for whom the very fact of annihilation is the promise of a rebirth in some new dimension. Sometimes the Beckett hero seems strangely close to this inconceivable transmutation (*Murphy*, *The Unnamable*), sometimes Hell seems scarcely an instant away (*Endgame*, *Textes pour rien*): but, without exception, Purgatory is the residence of every different manifestation of Beckett's *moi*: it is the home of Man.

Characteristically, Beckett's first hero (or rather antihero: there is nothing conventionally heroic about any of "my people," as he himself likes to think of them; one and all are artists in the art of failure) is drawn from Purgatory direct. When Dante placed his classic procrastinator, Belacqua, beneath a rock below the Gates of Purgatory, there to relive in mind and dream all the days and instants of his life before the gates would open—

> Prima convien che tanto il ciel m' aggiri
> di fuor da essa, quanto fece in vita,
> perch' io indugiai al fine i buon sospiri[5]—

it is unlikely that he foresaw the reincarnation of his some-time Florentine acquaintance in the guise of a down-at-heel Irishman—student, poet, clown, seducer—amid a people who would gleefully distort his name to "bollocky." Belacqua Shuah, "a dirty low-down Low Church Protestant"[6] of Huguenot stock, likewise lives out his life in indolence beneath the shadow of his "rock" —which, in the event, proves to be a more-than-doubtful public house in Lombard Street, Dublin. The ten stories of *More Pricks than Kicks* (1934) are uneven in quality but they already bear to a remarkable degree the hallmarks of Beckett's art. They range from the cruel and bitter brilliance of "Dante and the Lobster," by way of the oddly disturbing overtones of "Ding-Dong" and an unforgettable parody of love in the German manner ("The Smeraldina's Billet-Doux") to the rather dated and mannered satire of "A Wet Night" and "What a Misfortune!" Taken as a whole, they trace in sequence the disquieting career of Belacqua Shuah, from his early Italian lessons with Signorina Ottolenghi and through his three successive marriages, to his drearily accidental demise and solemn burial. The stories, as stories, are adequate; but each one is transcended by the total personality of Belacqua.

Belacqua bears all the authentic marks of Beckett's "people." Idle by conviction as well as by temperament, his inactivity is a positive statement of his essential existence. Between the great granite slabs which are reality, ambition, competence, there are small black interstices of nothingness—and these are Belacqua's life. He lives, he says, "a Beethoven pause"[7]—and then derives the greatest satisfaction from his inability to explain precisely what he means. Even in his love-making he somehow manages, most of the time, to dodge the realities of sex and to evaporate into some crevasse of unreality, accessible to none but himself. Indeed, for Belacqua, the act of love is the supreme symbol of failure —the failure which pertains necessarily to the condition of man while man remains the pathetic anomaly he is, a scrap of life surrounded by death, a something encircled by nothing. There is no escape into some super-existence of ideal love, into the "music" of Platonic perfection. If there *is* a solution to the problem of mortality—and all Beckett's work from beginning to end is concerned with hunting for such a solution—it lies, not in "transcending" death, but in discovering a dimension of life which reduces death to an inane irrelevance. The search which Beckett undertakes is for a *continuity* of existence, in which death is but a scarcely-noticed incident—the same insignificant, unnoticed incident which lies between *Malone Dies* and *The Unnamable*. And if eternity—all that lies on every side, beyond death as before life—is Nothing, then life itself must move into a dimension of Nothingness, if there is to be continuity. This, progressively, is what happens to Belacqua. Not the music, but the pauses between the music—these constitute Belacqua's world. Existence can take on a reality impervious to death only if it is *not* existence, in any accepted sense of the term. " 'What I am on the look out for', said Belacqua, 'is nowhere, as far as I can see'."[8] And yet this existence must, in one form or another, be something positive, or at least it must offer incontrovertible evidence of itself. "Where now? Who now? When now?" is the first anguished cry of The Unnamable; and the one unendurable platitude for any of Beckett's people is the casual "Ah! There you are!" "So there you are again!"

says Vladimir, unthinkingly. "Am I?" queries Estragon.[9] But this lesson in epistemological humility has already been taught to Belacqua by Signorina Ottolenghi, as he looks for his page in Dante:

> "Where were we?" said Belacqua.
> But Neapolitan patience has its limits. "Where are we ever?" cried the Ottolenghi, "Where we were, as we were. . . ."[10]

Life in the interstices of reality, however, poses certain urgent questions. To Belacqua, it seems that "reality"— that alien world which he fears and despises—is first and foremost something static, as static as his name-sake's rock in Ante-Purgatory. It follows therefore that Belacqua's interstitial existence will be, by definition, one of movement—of futile, purposeless movement, leading nowhere. Symbolically, his "ruined feet" are constantly in anguished motion; "even in the night, they took no rest, or next to none. For then the cramps took over from the corns and hammer-toes and carried on."[11] His "spavined gait" carries him incessantly from place to place; it takes him "from the ingle to the window, from the nursery to the bedroom . . . and back."[12] And when he moves out of doors, he follows the motion of a boomerang thrown haphazard, and finishes up at his original starting-point, having accomplished precisely nothing:

> He was pleased to think that he could give what he called the Furies the slip by merely setting himself in motion. [. . . .] The mere act of rising and going, irrespective of whence and whither, did him good. That was so.[13]

Unhappily, however, the attribute of motion is indissociable from that of time, and to live within time is to live within the boundaries of mortality. And so Beckett's people, having started, like Belacqua, in constant motion, tend more and more, like Malone and The Unnamable, above all like Winnie in *Happy Days*, towards a total immobility, a *stasis* from which all motion, and consequently all time, is gradually excluded. Yet Belacqua, prophetic in so many ways, contrives to find something of timelessness, even in his incessant motion. His aimless peregrinations, by the very fact of their purposelessness, defeat reality, and thus somehow appear to evade the grasp of time. His watch stops. The striking of a clock is torture to him. His very movement is the gap in reality, the "Beethoven pause," which constitutes his living approximation to the Void. It is "a moving pause," as he himself defines it. Already with Belacqua we are plunged headlong among the paradoxes which form the substance of Beckett's work. Belacqua is the first significant incarnation of Beckett's *moi*.

Like Beckett, he is a poet and a Dubliner; like Beckett, a scholar, a student of Italian, a lover of Dante; and the landscapes and townscapes amongst which he conducts his erratic and futile excursions are those of Beckett's own childhood. The Leopardstown racecourse is destined to reappear in the Beckettian dream-world, when Watt spots it from the train on his way to the house of Mr Knott; and the little railway-station, where Watt takes his final ticket "to the further end of the line"[14]— perhaps the same as that where Maddy Rooney comes to meet her Dan in *All That Fall*—could well be that of Foxrock. At Foxrock, south of Dublin, Mr and Mrs Otto Olaf bboggs long for "a home of their very own";[15] and at Foxrock, in 1906, Samuel Beckett himself was born.

He was the son of a quantity-surveyor, and came of Protestant Irish middle-class stock. (A number of his "people" likewise have solid *bourgeois* backgrounds, which they contemplate with unadulterated loathing: Belacqua refers succinctly to "the incontinent bosthoons of his own class.") He was brought up strictly, "almost a quaker," in his own phrase, and sent, at the age of fourteen, to Portora Royal School at Enniskillen. In 1923, he went

up to Trinity College, Dublin, where he read French and
Italian, and took his degree in 1927. And in 1928 he went
to Paris.

The École Normale Supérieure in the rue d'Ulm has on
its staff two "lecteurs d'anglais," and these, by tradition,
are chosen from among the most brilliant newly-
graduated students of French, one from Oxford, the other
from Trinity College. For two years, Beckett held one of
these much-coveted posts, and almost immediately he
plunged into the literary life of Paris. This was the period
when Eugène Jolas was publishing *Transition*, while James
Joyce and his band of willing acolytes were struggling
with the early versions of *Work in Progress*, later to be
known as *Finnegans Wake*. To this circle, Beckett rapidly
attached himself; he would sometimes read aloud to the
Master, who was nearly blind, sometimes annotate
learned works for him; and, together with Alfred Péron,
he produced a French translation of the "Anna Livia
Plurabelle" episode in *Finnegans Wake*.[16]

Many critics have been misled by this association between Joyce and Beckett, and have assumed both an
intimacy and an influence greater than the evidence will
allow. The relationship was complex, and at times dis-
tinctly uncomfortable on both sides. At its best, it led to
serious communal work-sessions with Paul Léon, Eugène
Jolas, Ivan Goll, and Joyce himself, to such bacchic
occasions as the "déjeuner Ulysse," with Paul Valéry,
Jules Romains, Adrienne Monnier, and Léon-Paul
Fargue,[17] or to the fruitful silences of companionship.
But all was not harmony, nor was Joyce invariably wel-
coming. "Though he liked having Beckett with him,"
reports Ellmann, "Joyce at the same time kept him at a
distance. Once he said directly, 'I don't love anyone
except my family', in a tone which suggested, 'I don't
like anyone except my family either'."[18]

The many-sidedness of this relationship, its disappoint-
ments as well as its delights, must be taken into account

in any attempt to assess Joyce's influence on Beckett as a writer. That there *was* such an influence is undeniable. Not only did Beckett publish a fragmentary "Text" in the manner of Joyce, but he also wrote a learned and involved essay entitled "Dante . . . Bruno. Vico . . . Joyce," which was published in 1929 and held pride of place in a volume whose strange title was probably the work of Joyce himself: *Our Exagmination Round His Factification For Incamination Of Work In Progress*. There are traces of Joycean style (particularly from the later chapters of *Ulysses*) in *More Pricks than Kicks* and in *Watt*; on the other side, the Master seems greatly to have appreciated *Murphy*,[19] while characteristically misunderstanding its purpose from beginning to end. Certainly Beckett is as Irish as Joyce, as learned as Joyce, and—in *Watt* at least—as irreverent as Joyce. But there the likeness ends, even though some illusory appearances of similarity continue.

Like Joyce, he is intrigued by words, but whereas, for the author of *Finnegans Wake*, language was an intimate part of the mystery of creation, for Beckett words are the chief ingredient of the art of failure; they form that impenetrable barrier of language which forever keeps us from knowing who we are, what we are. Like Joyce, he is fascinated by numbers: but Beckett's calulations have none of that woolly-minded, pseudo-mystical significance which Joyce attached, say, to the number 1132; Beckettian mathematics are rungs on the ladder which leads towards a rationalistic assault on the inconceivable or the infinite. Joyce exploited his learning and continually increased it—"the more he knew, the more he could"—whereas Beckett has renounced his claim to erudition. The main theme of his work is impotence, of mind just as much as of body. All Beckett's tramps are erstwhile scholars, but, like Vladimir, and Estragon, they "have waived their rights," and their scholarship, like Winnie's "classics," belongs irrevocably to the past. Belacqua and

Murphy still carry a portion of their learning about with them, but Watt has already discarded it; and even in *Murphy*, the main function of Beckett's immense personal achievement in scholarship is to suffer a grotesque transmutation into pedantry, and so to furnish the predominant element of his humour and his comic style. Joyce was an encyclopedist; Beckett is an academic clown, who achieves his effects by applying the minute, unhurried and painstaking exactitude of a Michael Ventris deciphering Linear B to the problem of eating a packet of five mixed biscuits in the most satisfactory order.

In spite of their superficial resemblances, Joyce and Beckett are in reality poles apart; and *The Unnamable*, all in all, probably owes as much, if not more, to Pascal's *Pensées*, as to *Finnegans Wake*. Pascal's awareness of the Nothingness of man in the context of the silence of infinite space, his desperate groping after the elusive insubstantiality of self (compare his *Qu'est-ce que le moi?*[20] with *The Unnamable*), his despairing trust in a ratiocinative method which he knows can lead only to irrational conundrums, his *angoisse* in the face of what he cannot conceive and yet must conceive if he is not to despair for ever—all these experiences are all too familiar to Beckett. Pascal's title, *Misère de l'Homme sans Dieu*, would cover everything that Beckett has written. But Pascal, after his conversion, had a neat answer to the problem; whereas Beckett, if he too has an answer, a sort of answer, finds it in a domain of ideas more complex than Pascal ever dreamed of.

In 1931, Beckett was appointed to a Lectureship in French at Trinity College—a post which he resigned within a year, on the grounds that "he could not bear the absurdity of teaching to others what he did not know himself." After this came the *Wanderjahre*, in London, in France, and in Germany, but finally, in 1937, he settled in Paris, where he has remained ever since, save for brief visits to Ireland and a spell in the Vaucluze, in hiding from the Gestapo. In 1938, he began to write poetry in

French, and, from 1945 onward, prose also; and most of the works upon which his fame is based — the *Nouvelles*, the *Trilogy*, *Godot*—were written in that language during a concentrated period of six years, from 1945 to 1951.

Beckett's reasons for turning to French are by now fairly clear. The peculiar characteristics of English as a language are, firstly, its comparative freedom from grammatical rigidity, and secondly, the extraordinary powers of sensory evocation possessed even by the most insignificant of words. In English, the words do half the poet's work for him, and the temptation is to let them do more and more, to let them take over directly from a subconscious which gives the impulse but which does not direct, and for the writer merely to follow whithersoever the whim of language wanders.

There is much of this in Beckett's early poems:

> grave suave singing silk
> stoop to the black firmament of areca
> rain on the bamboos flower of smoke alley of
>   willows . . .[21]

and so long as the subject-matter remains on the whole deliberately commonplace, earthy and "real" (which, all in all, is true of *Echo's Bones*), the independent creative powers of language are a valuable asset. But gradually Beckett's purpose changes. His subject-matter begins to drift further and further away from the realms of common "reality" towards that Nothingness which is ultimate reality. And the Nothing is that which, by definition, *cannot* be expressed directly in terms of language. All language, therefore, is specious, and the independent language of poetry, the most dangerous and misleading of all. Beckett, in the final analysis, is trying to say what cannot be said; he must be constantly on his guard, therefore, never to yield to the temptation of saying what the *words* would make him say. Only when language is, as it were, defeated, bound hand and foot; only when it is so rigorously disciplined that each word describes exactly and quasi-scientifically the precise concept to which it is related and no other, only then, by the progressive elimination of that which precisely *is*, is there a remote chance for the human mind to divine the ultimate reality which *is not*. And this relentless, almost masochistic discipline, which reaches its culmination in *Comment c'est*, Beckett achieves by writing in a language which is not his own—in French.

To Herbert Blau, Beckett confided that French "had the right weakening effect"; to Niklaus Gessner, that "in French it is easier to write without style"; to myself, that he was afraid of English "because you couldn't help writing poetry in it." This last explanation perhaps offers a clue also to one of the more puzzling riddles in Beckett's writing—namely, that whereas much of his prose is superb poetry, most of his "poetry" is second-rate verse.

In 1930, the Hours Press in Paris announced a prize of £10 for the best poem on the subject of Time, the judges to be Richard Aldington and Nancy Cunard. Beckett submitted a composition entitled *Whoroscope* . . . and won. The hero of the poem is Descartes (of whom more later); the subject, Time the Harlot, from the egg—

> What's that?
> A little green fry or a mushroomy one?
> Two lashed ovaries with prostisciutto?
> How long did she womb it, the feathery one?
> Three days and four nights?
> Give it to Gillot.[22]

—to the tomb; the manner so hermetic, that the author himself is obliged to supply some two pages of footnotes, and the reader is still left largely in the dark.

It is undeniable that these poems in English, *Whoroscope* and *Echo's Bones* (1935), already contain many of Beckett's later themes in embryo, provided that one has the patience to dig for them. Above all, there is the reiterated theme of death—

> Exeo in a spasm
> tired of my darling's red sputum
> from the Portobello Private Nursing Home . . .[23]

—and its corollaries, those burning questions which appear between the lines in every page that Beckett has written:Can I forgive God for not existing? And if he did exist, could I forgive him for the suffering which he inflicts on man? None the less despite their irony, their thematic compression and their very personal, staccato rhythms, these poems are essentially museum-pieces. Their French successors, watery reflexions of Verlaine and Mallarmé, are still less impressive. And yet this same Beckett, whose poetry seems to be that of his own Belacqua, has only to turn to prose in order to obtain some of the most haunting and unforgettable effects in the language:

> ESTRAGON: All the dead voices.
> VLADIMIR: They make a noise like wings.
> ESTRAGON: Like leaves.
> VLADIMIR: Like sand.
> ESTRAGON: Like leaves . . .[24]

One explanation would seem to be that Beckett's themes are so complex and so intangible that they require elaboration on a vast scale; condense them to this:

> what would I do without this world faceless
>   incurious
> where to be lasts but an instant where every
>   instant
> spills in the void the ignorance of having been
> without this wave where in the end
> body and shadow together are engulfed . . .[25]

—and the result is something very like banality. But there is perhaps a subtler reason for Beckett's failure as a writer of poetry. Among all the poems, the best (with the important exception of the incidental poems in *Watt*) is undoubtedly *Whoroscope*, and it is at least possible that the reason for this is that *Whoroscope* alone introduces a "narrator." The "I" of *Whoroscope* is not Beckett himself, but Descartes. It may be that one of the keys to the whole of Beckett's art is his intense and by now almost proverbial shyness, his fear of revealing himself to the jeers of the Philistines. Consequently, in his poetry, where he usually speaks directly, he either camouflages his Self so well that none but his intimates can guess at the hidden meanings, or else reduces this same Self to a commonplaceness which even the *Figaro Littéraire* might find acceptable. In *Whoroscope*, however, he has interposed between himself and the world another figure, and this is the solution which will be continued in *Murphy* and *Watt*, in the un-published *Mercier et Camier*, and in the plays—with this additional factor, that Murphy, Watt, etc., are also grotesque, and the element of parody serves as an additional barrier against the ironic assaults of the world. But the final solution—arrived at gradually by way of *Molloy* and *Malone Dies*—lies in the creation of a pseudo-Self, a narrator whose "I" is at first reading indistinguish-able from Beckett's own, and yet who, clearly, moves in a dimension which is not that of any living mortal.

Beckett's "I" is a most ingenious invention. Its essen-tial function is that of object rather than of subject, a factor which permits him to take the study of the disinte-gration of personality beneath the impact of introspec-tion farther than it has ever been taken before; yet at the same time, it relates indirectly to himself. Its evolutions are those of an abstract philosophical system; but the *angoisse* which accompanies these evolutions is Beckett's own. It is still a "third person" between writer and reader but this third person has, as it were, become transparent —yet is none the less an independent entity, none the less not-Beckett for all that. And this supremely successful technique of the pseudo-Self was in all probability derived from Proust.

If the influence of Joyce, like that of Kafka, Leopardi, Dostoevsky, Schopenhauer, etc., is debatable, that of Proust lies beyond doubt. Beckett's short study of *Proust* (1931) is in itself a remarkable achievement. Its style is jejeune in the extreme, a tapestry of academic *bons mots* decorated with cornucopias of metaphors; however, discarding this tiresome verbiage and discounting the occasional platitude, *Proust* reveals itself, not only as one of the first really serious analyses in depth of *À la Recherche du Temps Perdu*, but as a sort of preview of almost all the main themes of Beckett's later work.

Essentially, what Beckett discovered in Proust, and later developed in his own writing, was an attempt to resolve the conflict between "awareness," which is instantaneous, and the linear extension in time of that same awareness when translated into language. Because words "take time," they are fundamentally ill-adapted to the task of defining any aspect of absolute reality, since all "reality"—in any metaphysical sense—is in the present, that is, is instantaneous. Proust believed that the human essence was endowed with an absolute reality outside time and space; whereas, in this life, it found itself imprisoned within time and space, denied even a full awareness of its own Self, since the only "Self" which it could conceive was compounded of memories accumulated by arbitrary selection from the past, and the "past," being forever beyond its grasp and comprehension, had no reality of its own. To escape from this tyranny of time, which actually annihilated the reality of the Self, Proust invoked the aid of "involuntary memory," and, much later, of art. Both, he believed, had the power to enable the subject to relive instantaneously in the present a total *sequence* of experience belonging to a past Self, thus enabling the true and extra-temporal Self to escape—

provisionally at least—from "that double-headed monster of damnation and salvation—Time."[26]

Proust's problem was, and still is, Beckett's problem; but Proust's solution failed to satisfy him in the long run. "Involuntary memory" is all very well (Nell has an experience of it in *Endgame*), but what has the past Self, even instantaneously recreated, to do with the Self now, in the inconceivable present? Are not both, in any case, compounded equally of words? And what is "art"? An ineffable and extra-temporal mystery? Or rather a supremely competent technical accomplishment in the rat-race for "possessing"? The only art which Beckett recognises—we saw earlier—is the art which escapes its "bourgeois" origins by attempting the impossible: the art which *must* fail. And so, from *Murphy* onwards, we find him everlastingly in search of new solutions to the Proustian riddle: How am "I," an a-temporal being imprisoned in time and space, to escape from my imprisonment, when I *know* that outside space and time lies Nothing, and that "I," in the ultimate depths of my reality, am Nothing also?

Other themes likewise emerge from this study of Proust: the discontinuity of personality, the failure of love and friendship, the failure of communication, the necessary solitude of the artist, the belief that suffering is the one force powerful enough to establish, even in the teeth of Time, the identity of the Self. In particular, however, it is in *Proust* that we find the first signs of that futile yet unquenchable revolt against the arbitrary factors of existence, which rises to the surface in *Watt* and finally comes to dominate so much of Beckett's thought— a revolt against the intolerable imprisonment of the sentient being within the determinism of cause and effect, of beginning and ending, of being obliged to end because something else is beginning, or obliged to begin because something else is ending; the anguished rebellion of the spirit against the insensate and meaningless limitations imposed upon it—the compulsion of birth, the worse compulsion of death—by a cosmos which is not to be forgiven merely because it knoweth not what it doeth. "The mortal microcosm cannot forgive the relative immortality of the macrocosm," writes Beckett solemnly in *Proust*, and then, with a flash of inspiration which illuminates all his work,

"The whisky bears a grudge against the decanter."[27]

REFERENCES

1. *W.F.G.*, pp. 42–4.
2. *Transition Forty-Nine*, No. 5, pp. 97–103.
3. *Op. cit.*, p. 101.
4. *N.T.P.R.*, p. 141.
5. Dante, *Purgatorio*, Canto IV, lines 130–2.
6. *M.P.T.K.*, p. 249.
7. *Op. cit.*, p. 45.
8. *Op. cit.*, p. 193.
9. *W.F.G.*, p. 9.
10. *M.P.T.K.*, pp. 17–18.
11. *Op. cit.*, p. 10.
12. *Op. cit.*, p. 43.
13. *Ibid.*
14. *W.*, p. 270; cp. *M.P.T.K.*, p. 141.
15. *M.P.T.K.*, p. 165.
16. Beckett's translation is quoted in Philippe Soupault, *Souvenirs de James Joyce*, 1943, pp. 73–81.
17. 27 Jun. 1929. See Richard Ellmann, *James Joyce*, 1959, pp. 628–9.
18. Ellmann, *op. cit.*, p. 661.
19. See Ruby Cohn, "Preliminary Observations," 1959. Also Ellmann, *op. cit.*, pp. 714–15.
20. Pascal, *Pensées*, Art. V, No. XVII.
21. From "Alba," *Poems in English*, p. 23.
22. From "Whoroscope," *Poems in English*, pp. 8–12.
23. From "Enueg I," *Poems in English*, p. 18.
24. *W.F.G.*, p. 62.
25. *Transition Forty-Eight*, No. 2, p. 97.
26. *Proust*, p. 1.
27. *Op. cit.*, p. 10.

CHAPTER II

BAROQUE RATIONALISM

"To confront the limits of the human condition," writes Martin Esslin, "is not only the equivalent of facing up to the philosophical basis of the scientific attitude, it is also a profound mystical experience." Beyond the questions which *can* be answered in terms which the human reason can grasp and use, lie others, whose very formulation is often beyond the limits of language, and whose answers may be supra-rationally apprehended, but never rationally expounded. What am I? What are time and space? What are mind and matter, what is reality? These are the questions which form the substance of Beckett's first novel, *Murphy* (1938), and which Beckett has been asking over and over again ever since; but the uniqueness of Beckett's people lies in the fact that they are resolved to supply an answer, not in terms of some facile mysticism of the take-it-or-leave-it variety, but in terms of a coherent rationalism which, strictly speaking, denies them the right even to formulate such questions, and whose validity as a method would be irrevocably annihilated, were the answers to be found. This is one of the factors which sets Beckett apart from the writers of the Absurd. For "the Absurd" is a method which proceeds, by means of the annihilation of rational concepts, to a point where ultimate reality, irrational by definition, may be glimpsed through the wreckage. But Beckett, by contrast, cherishes rationality above all things, but drives it to the point at which—just as moving particles are transformed as they approach the speed of light—reason itself is transmuted into the still vaster reality of the irrational.

Murphy is a "nihilist" in the most literal sense of the word: that is to say, he is not a moral cynic, still less a revolutionary iconoclast of the Bazarov type, but simply a being whose whole outlook, life and philosophy is based upon *das Nichts*. Murphy in his rocking-chair finds what Belacqua found in his aimless peregrinations through the streets of Dublin, the timeless Void of absolute existence; but over and above this, Murphy has "expectations." The Proustian phenomenon of "involuntary memory" combines in Murphy with the Belacqua-theme of Dante's vision, and Murphy believes—admittedly without much evidence—that the ephemeral freedom of his rocking-chair will, by the act of death, be transformed into a total freedom in which his Self, redeemed at last from pastness and futurity, will relive in an instantaneous present, eternally extended into timelessness, the whole of his mortal existence. This awareness of a possible and final escape from time, Murphy terms his "Belacqua fantasy"—a grotesque invention which is none the less the key to the novel of which he is the hero:

At this moment Murphy would willingly have waived his expectation of Antepurgatory for five minutes in his chair, renounced the lee of Belacqua's rock and his embryonal repose, looking down at dawn across the reeds to the trembling of the austral sea and the sun obliquing to the north as it rose, immune from expiation until he should have dreamed it all through again, with the downright dreaming of an infant, from the spermarium to the crematorium. He thought so highly of this post-mortem situation, its advantages were present in such detail to his mind, that he actually hoped he might live to be old.[1]

Murphy is actually in his rocking-chair "of undressed teak, guaranteed not to crack, warp, shrink, corrode, or creak at night," when first we meet him. Like Belacqua, he is a sometime scholar and student (of theology, in this instance), half clown, half pedant, a vagabond Irishman washed up in London, with a strong aversion to work and a complete absence of material ambition. He is the searcher after infinity, but infinity is *his* infinity, it is the infinite dimension of his own Self, his "precious ipsissimosity," to use Belacqua's phrase, and other people are no more than obstacles to his eventual self-realisation. Other people need Murphy, but Murphy needs no one—not even Celia, who loves him, and whom his body, to his fine disgust, desires. Celia, a gentle Irish prostitute with a beat in the region of Cremorne Road, Battersea, is the only woman in the whole of Beckett's work who is delineated with love and tenderness. This quasi-pastoral idyll, however, comes to grief on the hard rocks of finance. "Celia spent every penny she earned, and Murphy earned no pennies."[2] So in desperation she goads him into doing that which is most abhorrent to his nature: looking for a job.

So repugnant to Murphy is the prospect of immersing himself in the gross reality of life around him, that even death from starvation seems infinitely preferable to work; but eventually, thanks to a chance encounter in a café with a revolting creature by the name of Austin Tickle-penny, providence sends him the one situation which fits his temperament—assistant male nurse at the "Magdalen Mental Mercyseat," as the local lunatic asylum is entitled. Here, among those fortunate misfits, whose carefully-nurtured rationality has led them, not outwards, but inwards towards implacably irrational conclusions, Murphy finds a kind of paradise on earth (Belacqua had already contemplated with envy the inmates of the Portrane Lunatic Asylum); and here he might have lived out happily the rest of his natural life, his nights spent in symbolic games of chess with Mr Endon ("voted by one and all the most biddable little gaga in the entire institution,"[3]) his days "at peace" in his cell-like garret, had not some farcical confusion between the respective purposes of a lavatory-chain and the switch of a gas-fire afforded him an appropriately purposeless demise—a demise which, as he passes in rapid succession through the differently graded blisses of contemplation, might *almost* be a parody of the death of the Buddha. Celia, like some shabby Pauline jilted for a martyrdom by her Grock-like Polyeucte, remains behind to take up the search where Murphy had laid it down, while the cremated ashes of her lover are scattered by accident over the floor of a low-class pub:

> By closing time, the body, mind and soul of Murphy were freely distributed over the floor of the saloon; and before another dayspring greyened the earth had been swept away with the sand, the beer, the butts, the glass, the matches, the spits, the vomit.[4]

The depth and brilliance—and humour—of this first novel do not lie in the story (which is further complicated by the machinations of a quartet of Dublin grotesques: Neary, Wylie, Neary's "*âme damnée* and man-of-all-work" Cooper, and the ineffably refined Miss Counihan, all "needing" Murphy for purposes of their own), but rather in a multiplicity of insignificant incidents and parentheses, and of course in Murphy himself. The symbol of Murphy's search for Nirvana is the closed circle: he is within himself a perfect (or nearly perfect) microcosm; he is a "closed system," by contrast with "the big blooming buzzing confusion"[5] of the outside world; he returns invariably upon himself, like Mr Endon's game of chess. But just as, in scholastic philosophy, the microcosm is the perfect reflexion of the macrocosm, so Murphy includes within himself all that exists within the cosmic totality—and as he rocks himself into a trance of "peace," his microcosm becomes a gradual Void and allows him at last to "come out of his mind" and be at one with the infinite. This "one-ness with the Void," however, has nothing to do with mere unconsciousness. Nirvana, or

Nothingness, is a *positive* experience, only to be reached through the most concentrated of mental efforts. The game of chess with Mr Endon (Gk. ενδον = "within") is an agonising experience for Murphy, for by his play Mr Endon reveals that he is far more adept at fashioning a closed-circuit microcosm than is Murphy himself. With something like despair, Murphy drops his head on his arms in the middle of the chessmen, "which scattered with a terrible noise": but then at last

Murphy began to see nothing, that colourlessness which is such a rare postnatal treat, being the absence (to abuse a nice distinction) not of *percipere* but of *percipi*. His other senses also found themselves at peace, an unexpected pleasure. Not the numb peace of their own suspension, but the positive peace that comes when the somethings give way, or perhaps simply add up, to the Nothing, than which in the guffaw of the Abderite naught is more real. Time did not cease, that would be asking too much, but the wheel of rounds and pauses did, as Murphy with his head among the armies continued to suck in, through all the posterns of his withered soul, the accidentless One-and-Only, conveniently called Nothing.[6]

The temptation to interpret this in terms of a specific branch of mystical teaching—Taoist, Buddhist or Zen-Buddhist—is very strong, and it is perhaps not wholly misleading to do so, provided that one remembers that Beckett employs a great variety of arguments to reach his objective, and that this, the least rational, is consequently the least important.

Taoism is not, in any Western sense, a "religion." It is a "way of liberation," or in other words, simply a *method*, just as logic is a method. It is a way of apprehending the reality of the Self in relation to ultimate reality, and above all of detaching the Self from all those specious appearances of reality which cling to it. If the

Self is imprisoned in Time, it is because it cannot escape from desire; it "clutches at" life, at things, at people; it destroys the Unity of existence by using language, by defining, dividing, measuring and separating the elements of the material world around it. Only when the mind has ceased to desire and to define can it be at one with the Totality, only then can it begin to feel its own essential reality. This total liberation from desire is Nirvana; but *what* Nirvana is cannot be defined in any positive sense, for anything that is positively defined is, by the fact of definition, separated from the Totality, and therefore is not Nirvana. Nirvana can be conceived, not as what it is, but only as what it is not. It is *not* anything. It is Nothing. And yet—and no Taoist will question this—it is a *positive* reality, a "plenum Void." It is the Self, and it is what lies beyond the Self. There is no question of mere annihilation. To quote "Democritus the Abderite," who was no Taoist, but who arrived at an identical conclusion by a different path, "Nothing is more *real* than Nothing."

But if, according to pure Taoist or Buddhist teaching, Nirvana is that which cannot be desired, and can be attained only when all desires are laid to rest by death, later sages developed specific techniques of asceticism and contemplation by which the living being might sometimes achieve at least an intimation of the ultimate Nothingness. These are the meditation techniques of Yoga, Zen and Za-Zen, particularly as taught in China and Japan. And there is every probability that Murphy is deliberately using these techniques—the detachment from the world, the annihilation of desire, the hypnosis induced by "the brilliant swallow-tail of Mr Endon's arms and legs," the rocking-chair—in order to achieve his intimations of the Void. Even Neary seems to have been an adept, since he had learned, "after years of application somewhere north of the Nerbudda,"[7] to stop his heart "more or less whenever he liked and keep it stopped." Moreover, Murphy's mind, so carefully described as being made up "of light fading into dark, of above and beneath, but not of good and bad. [. . .] It felt no issue between its light and dark, no need for its light to devour its dark,"[8] conforms closely to the Buddha's view of the relation of good to evil in the universe. Indeed, there are other typically Beckettian symbols which allow, without too much stretching of the evidence, a similar interpretation. The "circle broken at its lowest point," which forms the subject of the mysterious painting in Erskine's room,[9] and the crawling chain of executioners and victims which is the theme of the final part of *Comment c'est*, both suggest the concept of Karma, the "wheel" of birth, death and reincarnation from which there is no escape save through Nirvana; Lucky's strange dance (derived in any case from the ritual dances of the Japanese Noh theatre), which he calls "the Net," could well be the "net of words and concepts" in which, according to Buddhist teaching, our ultimate Self is entangled; and finally, the stress which certain forms of Buddhism lay on contemplation in the sitting position (Za-Zen) could be the reason why Cooper, later Molloy and Moran, later still Hamm's servant Clov can lie or stand but never sit—their very bodies symbolising their exclusion from that pleasure, freedom and appeasement that came to Murphy in his rocking-chair: "such pleasure that pleasure was not the word."

But if there is unquestionably an element of contemplative mysticism in *Murphy*, there are other, more important influences which lead in the same direction, but by routes more readily accessible to the Western mind. Unlike Joyce, whose mysticism forms an integral part of his whole creative process, Beckett does no more than toy with Oriental thought, extracting from it precisely such ideas and symbols as he needs, and abandoning the rest. The experiences of The Unnamable, for instance, to any thoroughgoing exponent of Zen, would be blissful; to Beckett, they are torture. As a Buddhist, Beckett is, to say the least of it, unsatisfactory; but in revenge he is an excellent Cartesian.

The major themes and convictions of Beckett's work rarely appear on the surface; they lie hidden away behind a smoke-screen of parody and apparently disconnected symbols, and the clues to their existence are often no more than half-quotations, passing allusions or the intrusion of an unexpected name. Remembering that the subject of Beckett's first published poem was Descartes, however, these half-buried clues take on a significance. Take an utterly insignificant fact: the "dream of Descartes linoleum" which gruesomely decorates the floor of Miss Carridge's lodging-house, where Murphy lives;[10] yet from this futile piece of facetiousness run invisible links in all directions—to Neary, who is described improbably as "a Newtonian," in contrast to Murphy himself who lives "in a tumult of non-Newtonian motion"; to Miss Counihan, who, having once been in love with Murphy, still retains a few tattered memories of the *Discours de la méthode*—

"There is a mind and there is a body," said Miss Counihan.

"Shame!" cried Neary. "Kick her arse! Throw her out!"[11]

—a most adequate Newtonian retort; and finally to "Murphy's mind," that "large hollow sphere, hermetically closed to the universe without," in which there reside "the mental fact and the physical fact, equally real if not equally unpleasant. . . ."

Thus Murphy felt himself split in two, a body and a mind. They had intercourse apparently, otherwise he could not have known that they had anything in common. But he felt his mind to be bodytight and did not understand through what channel the intercourse was effected nor how the two experiences came to overlap.

He was satisfied that neither followed from the other. He neither thought a kick because he felt one nor felt a kick because he thought one. [. . .] However that might be, Murphy was content to accept this partial congruence of the world of his mind with the world of his body as due to some such process of supernatural determination. The problem was of little interest.[12]

The clue to Beckett's method of transforming himself from a philsopher into a novelist lies in this last sentence. For Murphy the problem may be "of little interest"; for Beckett it is of supreme importance. Descartes had posited a rigid dualism: a mind which was purely spiritual, a body which was purely material and indeed mechanical (in Beckett's universe, this Cartesian concept of an idealised corporeal mechanism repeatedly takes on the symbolic form of the "bicycle"[13]). But there was a snag. Descartes, in spite of his appeal to the "pineal gland" and its "animal spirits," was no more able than is Murphy, his spiritual descendant, to explain the action of mind upon matter; and on this rock the whole implicit positivism of classic rationalism foundered. It was left to the Cartesians of the second generation—Malebranche, Geulincx, Géraud de Cordemay—to propose alternative solutions; and these solutions, no longer positive but veering once again towards the mystery of the *Néant*, no longer classic but strangely and fantastically baroque, are those which Beckett adopts.

Malebranche is mentioned by name in *Comment c'est*;[14] Geulincx, with his "beautiful Belgo-Latin: *Ubi nihil vales, ibi nihil velis*," not only in *Murphy*, but also in *La Fin*;[15] and all the novels are penetrated by their arguments. This baroque Cartesian logic went thus: since mind and matter are totally different substances, it is absurd to imagine that mind can act upon matter. Mind simply does *not* act upon matter, and what appears to be an interaction ("I move my hand") is in fact a pure coincidence of two separate actions, each determined by the will of God. God wills that I should desire to move my hand, and in the same instant, God causes it to move. God alone, then, is the primary cause of all movement; my will is but an "occasional cause," whose relevance is nothing but an illusion. The laws of cause and effect are meaningless, all purpose is illusion; the mind of man is Nothing; the will of God is all.

For Malebranche, even the action of matter upon matter was a divine coincidence; but Arnold Geulincx (1624–69), who has gone down to history somewhat comically as the perpetrator of the system known as "Geulincx's Clocks," would have disputed this. In the interlude between Descartes and Geulincx, the physicists had discovered the law of the conservation of momentum, according to which the total quantity of motion in the world in any given direction is constant. (To Beckett, this discovery is Newtonian, not Cartesian; he therefore distorts its application with a genial sleight-of-hand and attributes it to Neary: the "quantum of wantum" which "cannot vary.") The action of matter upon matter, therefore, may be exempted from the miraculous intervention of the Divine Will; and so also, in Geulincx's view, may the operation of mind upon itself. It is the interaction of mind and body alone which requires the miracle of coincidence to explain it, and so Geulincx postulates the analogy of two clocks, both keeping perfect time. The clock of mind points to the hour, the clock of matter strikes; and to the inattentive observer, there is a causal link between the two. But in fact this is an illusion. Man's mind can act upon itself, and so within itself is absolutely free; but its action in the outside world is not its own, but God's: *Impossibile est ut is faciat, qui nescit quomodo fiat.*[16] The Self, therefore, is totally incapable of influencing the outside world in any way; its only scope and significance lie within itself—in introspection.

Thus Murphy, the perfect Geulincxian, is turned forever inward upon himself. *Amor intellectualis quo Murphy se ipsum amat* is the phrase which stands at the head of the now celebrated description of "Murphy's Mind," that bodytight hollow sphere of light and dark, from which need and desire alike are absent. Need and desire alike belong to the irrelevant outside world. The first result of this baroque rationalism, therefore, is to lead Murphy into a position where, in order to be *free*, he must desire nothing, need nothing whatsoever: "the freedom of indifference, the indifference of freedom, the will dust in the dust of its object, the act a handful of sand let fall."[17]

The Geulincxian logic, however, goes further. Murphy's mind—the only relevant reality—is already turned in upon itself, loves nothing but itself: but what is its value *in* itself? Or in other terms, why, out of the fifteen hundred-odd pages of "beautiful Belgo-Latin" that Geulincx wrote, did Murphy choose to remember this one quotation: *Ubi nihil vales . . . ?* In relation to the world outside, the mind is impotent and valueless; within itself, it has value only in relation to God—but God is precisely the one Geulincxian concept that Murphy omits from his cosmogony. Take God away, and Murphy's mind is . . . Nothing: a Nothing forever turned inward, enwrapt in contemplation of itself.

What then occasions this "partial congruence" between consciousness and act? To Murphy, it can only be "some process of supernatural determination." The significance of the "determination" we shall see later, in *Watt*: but it is the supreme and comic irony of *Murphy* that its hero, in place of God, resorts quite literally to the supernatural—in fact, to astrology, an art which Descartes had specifically rejected. Thus the wheel has come full circle, and the supremely rational *Cogito* leads directly to the "Swami in Berwick Market who cast excellent nativities for sixpence."

And yet . . . the one advantage of a Self whose essence

is the Nothing is that that Self is totally *free*. To reject a divine determinism in Geulincx's sense, and then replace it by an astrological determinism is too absurd—even for Murphy. So, neatly, he reverses the situation. "Between him and his stars no doubt there was a correspondence"; but in this correspondence (Malebranchian sense) he, not they, is the dominating figure:

> They were *his* stars, his was the prior system. He had been projected, larval and dark, on the sky of that regrettable hour as on a screen, magnified and clarified into his own meaning. But it was *his* meaning.[18]

Or else perhaps, in other words, it is Murphy's clock which points to the hour; the mechanism of the heavens merely strikes.

Nor, in the absence of Voltaire's Divine Watchmaker, do the two clocks keep such perfect time. Murphy, Watt, Molloy, even Vladimir and Estragon, live in a world where the will to perform a simple act is not always followed unquestionably by the act itself. Murphy's body is a constant stranger to him, and like Molloy he contemplates his feet and hands with a disturbed detachment, as though they did not strictly speaking belong to "him." Their motions are a coincidence, their simplest movements are a source of wonderment. As pure fictions of the mind they would be comprehensible; as facts, the correspondence of their motions with the will to move is almost unbelievable—and again and again, Beckett's people feel the need to analyse their simplest movements and *prove* what they are doing. Hence also the extraordinary manner in which Beckett's people walk—Watt, most strikingly:

> Watt's way of advancing due east, for example, was to turn his bust as far as possible towards the north, and at the same time to fling out his right leg as far as possible towards the south, and then to turn his bust as

far as possible towards the south and at the same time
to fling out his left leg as far as possible towards the
north . . . and so on, over and over again, many many
times, until he reached his destination, and could sit
down.[19]

Here, what is missing is precisely the flow of intention
from mind to body. What we observe is a series of actions,
grotesquely analysed, which, by an imperfect coincidence, add up to the intention of "walking" in Watt's
mind.

To return to *Murphy*, however, what is fascinating is
the extraordinary skill with which this abstruse and un-
grateful material is turned into a superlative comic novel.
Beckett achieves this by burying the metaphysical sub-
structure of the novel deep beneath its quite literal
application—and since the metaphysics are baroque, the
application is grotesque. Newton, the traditional
opponent of Descartes, starts from an assumption of the
reality of movement in the universe; consequently, the
"Newtonians" (Neary, Wylie, etc.) are constantly in
motion. They bombinate like molecules in a gas-jar;
they rush wildly "from Euston to Holyhead, from Holyhead to Dun Laoghaire" their characteristic position is
the vertical, the active. Murphy, by contrast, is only truly
himself when he is stationary and seated:

The sensation of the seat of a chair coming together
with his drooping posteriors at last was so delicious that
he rose at once and repeated the sit, lingeringly and
with intense concentration. . . .[20]

—and even so, this is a compromise with the conventions;
what he really desires is "the long flat rapture on his
back."[21]

Thus is the dreaming stance of Belacqua beneath his
rock transformed into a symbolic horizontal *stasis*, and
few of Beckett's major characters remain vertical for long.

They fall (Murphy, Pozzo), they lie (Malone), they roll (Macmann), they crawl (Molloy, or Bom); occasionally they sit (Hamm), or, legless, are propped up in jars (Mahood); and sometimes, most characteristically of all, they prop themselves up rigid against a wall, thus forming the hypotenuse of a right-angled triangle, and thereby reducing the Cartesian machine to what by rights it should be: a simple formula in plane geometry. The tireless activity of Neary, Wylie & Co. reflects the functioning of the normal concept of the human mind, a mind constructed "on the correct cash-register lines, an indefatigable apparatus for doing sums with the petty cash of current facts."[22] But Murphy's mind is of a different cast: "It functioned not as an instrument but as a place, from whose unique delights precisely these current facts withheld him." A *place*: the tight-enclosed arena where, like some wrapt Cartesian Buddha, his well-disciplined reason contemplates in timeless ecstasy the Nirvana of the Self.

Inevitably, moreover, the microcosm seeks its equivalent in the macrocosm; and so Murphy's whole existence is an attempt to realise in the outer world an equivalent of the "hollow sphere" which is his mind, and to construct "his own little dungeon-in-Spain." His garret at the Magdalen Mental Mercyseat all but fulfils these metaphysical requirements; but finally it is the padded cells which offer an incomparable vision of bliss:

> The tender luminous oyster-grey of the pneumatic upholstery, cushioning every square inch of ceiling, walls, floor and door, lent colour to the truth, that one was a prisoner of air. [. . .] The compartment was windowless, like a monad. [. . .] Within the narrow limits of domestic architecture he had never been able to imagine a more creditable representation of what he kept on calling, indefatigably, the little world.[23]

This "little world" which Murphy inhabits is egotistical, anti-social, and by definition unloving and unlovable. Yet Celia loves Murphy; and Murphy, even despite himself, loves Celia. This is the strangest element in the novel, the most moving and the most irrational. For the first and last time, Beckett admits a supra-rational relationship, over and beyond the nihilistic arguments of reason. It is the "music" which lies beyond words, the "music, *music*, MUSIC . . . Celia, serenade, nocturne, albada,"[24] which passes even the Geulincxian understanding. It is futile. It is destructive. It lacks the simplest means to express itself. It gives nothing, neither happiness nor self-realisation. And yet it exists:

"At first I thought I had lost him because I could not take him as he was. Now I do not flatter myself."

A rest.

"I was a piece out of him that he could not go on without, no matter what I did."

A rest.

"He had to leave me to be what he was before he met me, only worse, or better, no matter what I did."

A long rest.

"I was the last exile."

A rest.

"The last, if we are lucky."

So love is wont to end, in protasis, if it be love.[25]

Not for another twenty years will Beckett allow the intrusion once again of this non-baroque irrationalism—the tenderness of heart that embraces even the Nothingness of Self.

REFERENCES

1. *Murphy*, pp. 77–8.
2. *Op. cit.*, p. 19.
3. *Op. cit.*, p. 240.
4. *Op. cit.*, p. 275. James Joyce once flattered Beckett by quoting this passage by heart. See Ellmann, *op. cit.*, p. 714.

5. *Murphy*, p. 4.
6. *Op. cit.*, p. 246.
7. *Op. cit.*, p. 3. The Nerbudda, or Narmada, is a river north of Bombay.
8. *Op. cit.*, p. 108.
9. *W.*, pp. 141–2.
10. *Murphy*, p. 140.
11. *Op. cit.*, p. 218.
12. *Op. cit.*, p. 109.
13. Not only for this interpretation, but for the main argument of this chapter I am heavily indebted to Prof. Kenner.
14. *C.C.*, p. 37.
15. *Murphy*, p. 178; *N.T.P.R.*, pp. 105–6; also *Molloy*, p. 51.
16. Geulincx, *Metaphysica vera et ad mentem peripateticam*, Amsterdam 1691, part 1, p. 5. Quoted by Mintz, "Beckett's Murphy," in *Perspective*, 1959, p. 158.
17. *Murphy*, p. 105.
18. *Op. cit.*, p. 183.
19. *W.*, p. 32.
20. *Murphy*, p. 80.
21. *Op. cit.*, p. 94.
22. *Op. cit.*, p. 178.
23. *Op. cit.*, p. 181.
24. *Op. cit.*, p. 252.
25. *Op. cit.*, p. 234.

CHAPTER III

WORDS AND NUMBERS

Watt is one of the most difficult, and at the same time one of the most brilliant novels that Beckett has written. It is difficult, but not in the sense that *The Unnamable* or *Comment c'est* are difficult—plotless novels, vast tapestries of words fitfully illuminating featureless "Selves" problematically existing in a fourth or fifth dimension. Watt lives and moves in *our* dimension, his life is the banal life of common Dublin folk. His background is made up of ordinary things: trams, local trains, canals, the Leopardstown racecourse, sunsets, houses, gardens, stairs, and stars. He has an unmistakable reality—a sordid, down-at-heel reality not unlike that of Murphy, who, aeons ago, he was; he still remembers those ancient constellations "which he had once known familiarly by name, when dying in London." He is "a very fair linguist" (all Beckett's people are). His past contains "two well-defined romances"; he is one of those "big bony shabby seedy haggard knock-kneed men, with rotten teeth and big red noses," and when first espied by Mr Hackett, propped up motionless in the twilight against a wall, he seems so perfectly integrated into the familiar world of Things, that he might have been "a parcel, a carpet for example, or a roll of tarpaulin, wrapped up in dark paper and tied about the middle with a cord." Yet somehow, wherever Watt exists, reality shifts oddly out of focus. Upon the friendly three dimensions of our lives, he imposes carefully his own, compounded out of words and numerals. And the numerals plunge headlong into the infinite, while the words lead straight to Mr Knott.

Or Not. Or Knot. Or Naught. Or Néant-Nichts-Nirvana, what you will.

Words are names for Things. The Thing, the *Ding-an-sich*, may well exist, or equally well may not, but while we have a word to name it, it exists for us, and we are safe. So also with people. Give Mr X—that indefinable Other, that alien Self—a name, and we can enclose him in our orbit, assimilate him, make him ours, familiar, harmless, three-dimensional. Our world begins with names:

> "My name is Spiro," said the gentleman.
> Here then was a sensible man at last. He began with the essential . . .[1]

—or, failing "proper" names, we can at least define the Thing as "Man":

> . . . a big fat yellow bun
> for Mr Man and a bun
> for Mrs Man and a bun
> for Master Man and a bun
> for Miss Man . . .[2]

—*M*an with a capital, M for Man, and M for Murphy, Micks, Molloy, Moran, Malone, Mahood, Macmann. . . . All Beckett's names have meanings, sometimes just Dickensian and ironic (Miss Fitt, Miss Carridge or Miss Rosie Dew), occasionally archetypal-clownish (Bim, Pim or Bom), more often names so dense with hypothetical suggestiveness, that we may choose and guess and argue as we please, and still come nowhere near reality. Godot, for instance. Or Hamm: Hamm, the ham-actor; the Hamlet, whose life is bounded in a nutshell—skull or cell—and yet might count himself king of infinite space, were it not that he had bad dreams; Hamm the Hammer, bearing down on Clov (Engl.: "clown" or "cloven." Fr.: *clou*, "a nail"), and Nell (another "nail") and Nagg (Germ.: *Nagel*, yet another "nail"). Or Mr Knott

(Germ.: *Not*, "need": what can Naught need?). Or Watt—or What? The answer—Not, or Knot, or Naught. A jungle of hypotheses, each leading, quite literally, no-where. For if the reality of man can be so much as guessed at, it can only be as a negative, or at best a question. Behind the name, the man; behind the man, the Void.

Murphy knew what his mind was; it had a form, or at least it admitted of description. Not so Watt. Watt's journey is a pilgrimage in search of meaning, and when first we meet him, he is outward bound. Driven by that obscure compulsion which all Beckett's people experience and accept, but which none can explain, he journeys to the house of Mr Knott, there to become a servant. In Mr Knott's house there are always two domestics: the new-comer, who serves the ground floor, and the old-estab-lished resident, who serves the upper floor which Mr Knott himself inhabits. When Watt arrives, Erskine, who previously has served the lower floor, moves up the stairs, while Arsène, who has earlier served the upper floor, moves out. And so Watt serves the lower floor. After a passage of time, however, a new servant arrives—Arthur. Relentlessly, the wheels of cause-and-effect revolve: Watt moves up the stairs, and Erskine vanishes. And then, one day, after yet another passage of time, Watt finds "in the kitchen a strange man sitting in the gloam-ing of the expiring range, on a chair"—as Watt himself had once sat. This man is called Micks. And so Watt's period as a servant in the house of Mr Knott comes to an end. Bag in hand and hat on head, he makes his slow way to the station, and takes the train, to nowhere in particular . . . to "the further end of the line." And when we meet him again (not later, but earlier, for time plays curious tricks) he is in an asylum, walking backwards, talking backwards, and in this devious manner trying to explain what happened when he lived with Mr Knott— his God, his ultimate, his *Nichts*:

Abandoned my little to find him. My little to learn
him forgot. My little rejected to have. To love him my
little reviled. This body homeless. This mind ignoring.
These emptied hands. This emptied heart. To him I
brought. To the temple. To the teacher. To the source.
Of nought.[3]

The novel, however, is not about Watt's actions. Its
true subject is Watt's mind, and the peculiarity of Watt's
mind is that it makes no intrinsic distinction between
words and objects. In short, Watt is a logical positivist, a
living incarnation of the theories of Fritz Mauthner[4] and
of Ludwig Wittgenstein. And the "tragic flaw in his
armour of logic and language"[5] appears when, in the
house of Mr Knott, he encounters a silence which is more
real and more significant than speech.

Wittgenstein's argument, reduced to its simplest terms,
is this: it is the human mind alone which divides up the
formless continuum of the universe into distinguishable
objects. The first characteristic of man is his ability to
identify, and in order to identify, he must have language.
To the child, all flowers are "flower" until it learns the
words for "buttercup" and "daisy." Where there is no
language, continues Wittgenstein, there is no thought;
and where there is no thought, there is nothing but the
massive, unidentified Totality of existence: there is All
and Nothing. There are words or . . . silence. "Wovon
man nicht sprechen kann," concludes the *Tractatus
logico-philosophicus*, "darüber muss man schweigen."

In other words, we can never hope to know anything
about phenomena; we can only know something about
the *words* relating to phenomena. Moreover, since language is the product of our own minds, it can never be
anything but arbitrary; on the other hand, it lies within
our power to make it at least as logical and as positive as
possible. Then at least we shall know precisely what our
words mean in relation to each other, even if we may

never know what they mean in relation to an ultimate reality.

If this is a scientific approach to language, then Watt is the supreme scientist of literature. His sensory evidence provides him with an awareness of phenomena; and once he has identified the phenomenon, found a word or words for it, and further, if the phenomenon is puzzling, shuffled around in the electronic computer of his mind all possible combinations of words which appear to relate to that phenomenon, then his knowledge is complete. The "meaning" of the phenomenon is exclusively the meaning of the words which "explain" the phenomenon; to seek for "meanings" in some mysterious or metaphysical domain beyond language is absurd. Beyond the word is Nothing.

For Watt, then, meaning and language are identical; and provided that he can formulate a statement in words about an event, he can dismiss it. It is "explained," and therefore harmless. What he cannot explain, he ignores—and must ignore—as literally meaningless. For Watt, there are material phenomena, and there is a linguistic mechanism called "mind" which manufactures "meaning." The notion that the meaning could actually reside in, or be involved with, the phenomena themselves, is inconceivable. And this is "comforting" to Watt. Nothing is mysterious, or frightening, or hostile, provided that the words are there to "explain."

But words are not absolute values in themselves. An explanation may be good and comforting, but another explanation may be equally good and equally comforting, and which of them is right? Since the mechanism of Watt's mind deals exclusively with linguistic logic— where one word is as good as another, and all are arbitrary—any one combination is as good as any other also; and if there are a dozen explanations, then the only resort is to give them all, knowing for certain, in consequence, that the "correct" one must be somewhere there among them. Another thing: the word-computer can only hope to function on condition that Watt gives it *all* the data, not merely a selection. This is the factor that accounts for the most extraordinary feature of *Watt*— the lists, the sequences, the merciless enumerations, the grotesque and exhaustive series of permutations and combinations of word-data which distinguish it from any other novel in the language. To Watt it seems perfectly clear that, given the *totality* of the relevant data, and given the leisure in his mind to reshuffle that data into every logically conceivable combination, there *must* emerge a verbally, and therefore logically, satisfying explanation. Not, of course, that this final explanation will ever actually "explain" anything—as is evident from the fantastic episode of Mr Knott's dog and Mr Knott's unfinished dinner. Watt's method is guaranteed to produce results which are flawlessly logical; at the same time, however, these results are wholly divorced, not merely from ultimate reality (whatever that may be), but also from common sense. By the end of the novel, Watt, with all his postulates and calculations, has said *nothing whatsoever* that is of the slightest relevance, either to himself or to Mr Knott. The "meaning" of each situation eludes him just as surely as it did before he started; none the less, by reducing the imponderables to language, he has contrived an exorcising explanation in a secondary dimension—and is thereby comforted:

He had turned, little by little, a disturbance into words, he had made a pillow of old words, for a head.[6]

Watt is the first incarnation of what is to be one of the primary themes of Beckett's later work: the failure of man, in his search for the significance either of himself or of the cosmos, to penetrate the barrier of language.

For practical purposes, in the unthinking round of daily life, Watt's method works well enough, since even Dubliners assume that the basis of reality is rational, and so can be reduced without distortion to the symbols of linguistic logic. But in Mr Knott's house, this is no longer true. Mr Knott, who is the only generating source of all "reality" within his own domain, is a Void; and as naught multiplied by any other number is still naught, the "other number" (*i.e.*, all that Watt *perceives* of Mr Knott and his surroundings) can vary to infinity, but the answer will still be the same: Nothing. And not only *can* vary, but does vary: the stairs, for instance,

> that never seemed the same stairs, from one night to another, and now were steep, and now shallow, and now long, and now short, and now broad, and now narrow, and now dangerous, and now safe. . . .[7]

In such a sum, the "other number" is irrelevant. No science, no logic can give it the power of altering the outcome, consequently it is always arbitrary and meaningless. Where (in Kantian terminology) the *Ding-an-sich* is a Void, the phenomena will be completely arbitrary. There will no longer be even the semblance of a rational necessity for their being, or continuing to be, as they are. And what is of its very nature irrational, cannot be grasped in language. So Watt's adventures in the house of Mr Knott are those of a man with a butterfly-net desperately trying to capture specimens, which, as soon as they are well and truly imprisoned, either slip through the meshes, or vanish altogether, or else transmute themselves into a different species. Watt's butterfly-net is language:

> Looking at a pot, for example, or thinking of a pot, at one of Mr Knott's pots, of one of Mr Knott's pots, it was in vain that Watt said, Pot, pot. Well, perhaps not quite in vain, but very nearly. For it was not a pot, the more he looked, the more he reflected, the more he felt sure of that, that it was not a pot at all. It resembled a pot, it was almost a pot, but it was not a pot of which one could say, Pot, pot, and be comforted.[8]

This is the beginning of Watt's *angoisse*. That which is not, cannot be assimilated to that which is, and the only positives in Mr Knott's domain are double-negatives, a point which Beckett makes stylistically throughout the novel. It is Watt's attempt to bring the irrational and the negative under the aegis of the rational and the positive that explains his horrified fascination with the episode of the Galls.

Few people call at Mr Knott's house, but among these rare visitors are "the Galls, father and son," who are come, as they explain, "all the way from town to choon the piano." They do so, under Watt's supervision, and, as they pack up to leave, exchange the following phrases:

The mice have returned, said Mr Gall Junior.

The elder said nothing. Watt wondered if he had heard.

Nine dampers remain, said the younger, and an equal number of hammers.

Not corresponding, I hope, said the elder.

In one case, said the younger.

The elder had nothing to say to this.

The strings are in flitters, said the younger.

The elder had nothing to say to this either.

The piano is doomed, in my opinion, said the younger.

The piano-tuner also, said the elder.

The pianist also, said the younger.[9]

The haunting quality of these phrases lies in the fact that they seem alternately meaningful and meaningless. As the scene continues "to unfold in Watt's head, over and over again," its total significance more and more eludes the grasp of rationality, just as each word spoken gradually empties itself of content. But in revenge it takes on a *form*, it develops "a purely plastic content"; it is transmuted into a kind of abstract art. Its meaning *is* its form, it is an art turned in upon itself, and owing its significance, not to "something" in the outside world to which it is related, but uniquely to its shape; it is "symbolic of itself"—"it became a mere example of light commenting bodies, and stillness motion, and silence sound, and comment comment."

This realisation which comes to Watt of a "meaning" which is not one of relationships (logic, or words related to things), but which exists in the absolute and therefore defies all formulation save in those terms in which it is already formulated—this is the greatest blow that Watt receives. With the Galls, he moves into a dimension where logic and language alike are helpless; there *is* no meaning, and yet there *has* to be a meaning. Like Beckett himself, Watt is compelled henceforward, armed with finite weapons, to grapple with the infinite; the *Néant* at the root of things has trapped him unawares and overwhelmed him.

Watt takes the exploration of *le Néant* a good deal further forward than *Murphy*. For Murphy, part rationalist, part mystic, the experience, even of his shabby, do-it-yourself Nirvana was blissful beyond description. In *Watt*, however, the mystic element has vanished, or nearly so. The Void is no longer a positive achievement, the answer to desire; it is approached by reason and discovered in the failure of reason—it is defeat, the bitter and anguishing defeat of human thought. Henceforward, in Beckett's work, the longing for the Absolute will never be free from terror. And this transition is made apparent in the character of Arsène.

When Watt comes in, by the effect of those immutable laws which govern Mr Knott's domain, Arsène goes out. But Arsène has lived long with Mr Knott, and as he leaves, gives Watt the benefit of his experience. His "short statement," incidentally, is an unbroken paragraph twenty-eight pages long, and constitutes the first of those great Beckettian monologues which, later on, are to form the substance of the *Trilogy*.

Arsène, less stubbornly perverse than Watt, chose early to relinquish all his intellect, his questions. He accepted from the outset the aura of Mr Knott's house for what it was: the Void, the centre which is also the Totality, the point without dimension which released the Self from its imprisonment in time and space, so that the isolation of the individual was dissolved in the "imminent Harmony" of the One. He who comes to Mr Knott's house, says Arsène, "will be in his midst at last, after so many tedious years spent clinging to the perimeter."[10] And Arsène is spiritually equipped to experience the full bliss of "a situation where to do nothing exclusively would be an act of the highest value and significance."

But then appears the reverse side of the medal. The Nothingness of Nirvana is *also* the Nothingness of the Absurd, and the transition from one to the other is both imperceptible and catastrophic. The first state lasts only "for a time"; it is a state of not-being and not-feeling, aware of Self yet unaware of pain or pleasure, unaware even of "the forgotten horrors of joy." Then suddenly, the Change:

> The change. In what did it consist? It is hard to say. Something slipped. [. . .] There is a great alp of sand, one hundred metres high, between the pines and the ocean, and there in the warm moonless night, when no one is looking, no one listening, in tiny packets of two or three millions the grains slip, all together, a little slip of one or two lines maybe, and then stop, all together, not one missing, and that is all, that is all for that night, and perhaps for ever that is all. . . .[11]

The "change" involved here is more than an awareness of the Absurd, in Roquentin's terms—more than an awareness of the invalidity of that rationalism, by means of which the irrational has been reached. It is an awareness that man can *never* escape his own rationality, and that his *Néant*—even when he is actually there—

involves a logical contradiction, and therefore cannot be. It is an impossibility, even when it exists. "What was changed, says Arsène, "was the existence of the ladder. Do not come down the ladder, Ifor, I haf taken it away."

This hoary Irish chestnut—which Beckett patriotically transposes into Welsh—is one of the key-symbols in the anti-logic of Nirvana. Arsène, for Watt's benefit, is trying to put the experience of Nothing into words—and realises the trap. For un-meaning cannot be discussed, still less defined, except in terms of meaning. One can only affirm that meaning does not exist in terms which imply that it does. To reach Negation (or "silence"), one must climb by the Wittgensteinian ladder of verbal affirmation:[12] but then, either the affirmations were nonsensical in terms of the ultimate negation; or else, if the affirmations persist, then the ultimate negation lies forever out of reach. Either the ladder does not exist, or else it can never be climbed to the top—and there you have "the logic of the joke."

So Arsène's argument continues. The very concept of Nirvana (non-meaning) implies, by Spinoza's law, the existence of a Something which is not Nothing. Nothing, therefore, engenders Something. But to engender cannot be the action of a negative: it is in itself a positive act. The very concept of the Nothing, therefore, destroys itself. Even the Buddha's thinking was merely incompetent. For if the Buddha taught that Nirvana was that which lay beyond desire, and therefore was that which could not be desired, the very fact of "not desiring" (retorts Arsène) asserts by implication the continued existence of desire:

It is useless not to seek, not to want, for when you cease to seek you start to find, and when you cease to want, then life begins to ram her fish and chips down your gullet until you puke, and then the puke down

your gullet until you puke the puke, and then the puked
puke until you begin to like it.[13]

Arsène's dense and difficult monologue is the most
explicit statement of Beckett's vision of the dilemma of
existence before *The Unnamable*. The *Trilogy*, in fact, is
little more than a detailed working-out of all the themes
that Arsène crams into the first few pages of his Jeeves-
like lucubrations. The rational cannot conceive the
irrational, save in terms of rationality; the human mind
is rational, the human Self is not. Therefore the one shall
never know the other.

There is, however, one last resort which Beckett's
people turn to—one last "ladder" which, more effec-
tively than words, holds out a promise to lead man from
the finite to the infinite without destroying the goal in the
ascent. This last resort is mathematics. The Beckettian
hero, even when he can no longer see nor speak, can still
count. "Not count!" mutters old Dan Rooney, incredu-
lously. "One of the few satisfactions of life!"[14]

In the earlier novels—*Murphy*, *Watt*, and *Molloy*
especially—the numeral tends to represent essence
stripped of existence, and consequently provides a step
towards that total freedom from the constriction of desire
which is the goal of Murphy and, to a lesser extent, of
Watt. When Murphy buys himself his packet of mixed
biscuits, "a Ginger, an Osborne, a Digestive, a Petit
Beurre and one anonymous," his total freedom, his experience of Nirvana, is limited by his sensual preferences.
"He always ate the first-named last, because he liked it
best, and the anonymous first, because he thought it very
likely the least palatable."[15] So long as the objects remained biscuits, and as such objects of desire or aversion,
he found that "these prepossessions reduced to a paltry
six the number of ways in which he could make his
meal." But reduce the phenomena to simple numerals
(1, 2, 3, 4, 5), and immediately the range of freedom is

extended, not infinitely as yet, but at least to the maximum of logically possible permutations of any five given
digits. Not only is this a maximum freedom within the
bounds of logic, not only is it escape from desire towards
the *Néant*, but even within the common experience of
living, the pleasures of variety are increased enormously.
Murphy is literally imprisoned by his "infatuation with
the Ginger"; transpose the assortment into a numerical
notation, and immediately it springs to life before him,
"dancing the radiant measure of its total permutability,
edible in a hundred and twenty ways!"

But the freedom of integers is nothing to the freedom
conferred by irrational numbers. Despite the fact that
numbers are less directly bound to "meanings" than
words, the system of rational numbers none the less ex-
presses a multitude of positive relationships in the visible
world. The sum: $2 + 2 = 4$ has "meaning" in the world of
sweets or apples. It has reality. But in the Belacqua-
interstices between these hard numerical realities lies the
mysterious world of incommensurables—numbers which
must exist (because they perform certain clearly-defined
functions in relation to other numbers), and yet do not
exist . . . which is impossible. The square root of 2, for
example. "Somewhere between $1\frac{169}{408}$ and $1\frac{70}{169}$ we may
expect $\sqrt{2}$ to exist, though we should not expect to find
it. But we can name it, know it is there, although it is
impossible."[16]

For Beckett, the irreducible decimal (π, or the
$52 \cdot 285714 \ldots$ of Watt's "mixed choir") is one of the
most obsessive symbols in his writing: it is the very image
of the human dilemma. Beckett's people themselves are
incommensurables—both in the sense that they are social
misfits, and also in the sense that they are "the extant
impossible." The Self, like $\sqrt{2}$, is that which exists, yet
cannot exist, performs known functions yet cannot be
known. To search for the Self is to search for the centre
of the circle—one may make ever-decreasing circles

round that centre, but the centre itself, being by definition dimensionless, can *never* be reached. We can approach the Self, in the same way as the recurring decimal can approach its end, for mathematically as well as metaphysically, the goal is identical: Zero. In the reduction of π, the figures after the point "accumulate, to no definite end, invariable patterns that grow less and less significant. And as their sum gradually approximates to the secret of the circle, their importance gradually diminishes towards zero."[17] So argues Professor Kenner, and, in one of the most illuminating studies of Beckett yet written, shows that Molloy (but it is equally true of all Beckett's people) is the incarnation of an irrational number, and belongs to that domain "which we can think about, but not enter with our minds":

For where Molloy could not be, nor Moran either for that matter, there Moran could bend over Molloy.[18]

There is, however, another side to the picture. As Beckett's people grow gradually more conscious of their graph-like extension towards the infinite, they become less and less tolerant of numbers which are merely finite. For Murphy, the 120 permutations of his biscuits represented a maximum of freedom within a finite system. But Watt, despite his obsession with permutability, is less readily convinced of what he can achieve with it.

For Watt himself is only too well aware that his ideal logical solutions to the problems he encounters in Mr Knott's house may well have no connexion at all with reality, and he is torn between two conflicting awarenesses: the one, of the arbitrary and illogical character of events as such; the other, of the inescapable framework of logic which is imposed on these events as soon as they are formulated in words. Language, in fact, imposes logic on events; and whereas the Absurd (the absolute-arbitrary quality of the instantaneous present), whatever its terrors, is at least a kind of freedom, the coherence of logical necessity appears to Watt more and more as an insupportable servitude.

It is this preoccupation which explains Watt's fascination with the "series." At first, Watt welcomes the concept of the series; he finds it "comforting," because the arbitrary and terrifying attributes of any given phenomenon can be explained away simply by assuming that present reality is no more than the "necessary product" of past circumstances. The phenomenon in isolation is inexplicable, meaningless and frightening; the phenomenon considered as the inevitable "effect" of a given "cause" is (apparently) meaningful, and therefore harmless. Admittedly, this does not resolve the problem altogether, because, in the first place, the entire chain of cause-and-effect, considered as a whole from the first origins of motion up to the present instant, is probably equally arbitrary (a "pre-established arbitrary," Watt calls it); and in the second place, because a cause in the *past* (which has no intrinsic "reality") does not suffice completely to remove all suspicion of arbitrariness from its effect in the very "real" present. None the less, Watt's first instinctive reaction is to "tame" the seemingly inexplicable by postulating a "series" of which any present phenomenon is merely a part.

As he penetrates deeper into the ambiance of Mr Knott's house, however, Watt grows less and less satisfied with this solution, for he begins to grow aware of a disquieting fallacy in the "law of cause and effect." Normally we think of "determinism" acting in one direction only—*i.e.*, the "cause" determines the "effect," but the "effect" does not determine retrospectively the "cause." There is a compulsion at one end, as it were, but freedom at the other—a reasonably satisfying compromise. But (Watt wonders) is this in fact the case? In any series (say, 4–5–6–7–8–9–10), if the position and nature of the effect are determined by the cause, the position and nature of the cause are equally limited by the effect. The attributes of 7, for instance, are determined by its predecessors 4-5-6: but they are just as severely limited by what they themselves determine, *i.e.*, the existence of 8-9-10. Every beginning determines the ending of that which preceded it, just as tyrannically as every ending determines a beginning. Within the series, there is not the thousandth part of a millimetre of freedom in *either* direction. The irrational number, then, is not merely a useful route towards infinity; it is the only possible alleviation of existence within the iron totalitarian régime of the integers.

Transpose this into *time*, moreover (which is what Watt does when he considers the curious laws governing the arrival and departure of Mr Knott's servants "Tom, Dick and Harry"),[19] and the necessary conclusion is that any event in a series is rigidly determined, not only by a chain of causes leading back into the remotest past, but also by a chain of effects leading forward into the infinite future ("from the long dead into the far unborn")— into a future which does not yet exist. It follows therefore, firstly, that that which is, is determined by that which is not, or at least that the present is determined by the future (*e.g.*, "Tom's two years on the first floor are *because of* Dick's two years on the ground floor . . ." which, to Watt, is "too horrible to contemplate"), and secondly that, the extension in time of every act being exactly predetermined with respect to its ending as well as with respect to its beginning, each act must fit exactly into a pre-allotted area in time:

For otherwise in Mr Knott's house, and at Mr Knott's door, and on the way to Mr Knott's door, and on the way from Mr Knott's door, there would be a languor and a fever, the languor of the task done but not ended, the fever of the task ended but not done, the languor and the fever of the going of the coming too late, the languor and the fever of the coming of the going too soon.[20]

But Watt, observing Mr Knott's house, concludes that this is not so. There is neither fever nor languor in Mr Knott's house. It follows therefore that there must be, in "Tom, Dick and Harry," some element which evades the "law of the series," while still remaining, to all appearances, embroiled in it. Over and above the structure of determinism ("the ordaining of a being to come by a being past, of a being past by a being to come"), there must also be, in every person if not in every act, a core of reality which is outside space and time, and which eludes the powers of space and time and logic to determine its existence. Not that Watt ever seriously questions the existence of this chain of determinism, but neither does he doubt the necessity for postulating an absolute and a-temporal existence in Tom, Dick and Harry. Yet neither of these postulates interests him very deeply in itself. What interests him is the one in relation to the other. For either Tom is temporal, in which case his whole existence is determined by his place in the series; or else he is a-temporal, a-spatial, and independent of the series —he cannot very well be both. *And yet,* says Beckett, *this is precisely what he is.* Human existence *is* a logical impossibility. It belongs to the series and yet evades the series; it is at once in time and out of time. For past and future alike belong to "the pre-established arbitrary": but the instantaneous present is both Nothing and Infinity.

And so Watt, in these strange pages that deal with "Tom, Dick and Harry," makes a first attempt to tackle what is to be the major theme of Beckett's later plays and novels: Time. But he tackles it still with limited materials —the four-square rationalism of the logical positivist. For Watt's tragedy is that he has no other tools at his command. The house of Mr Knott defeats him; the Void, the Infinite, destroys his armoury of words and arguments; yet at the end, when he has abandoned even the use of rational language:

> Deen did taw? Tonk. Tog da taw? Tonk. Luf puk saw? Hap! Deen did tub? Ton sparp. Tog da tub? Ton wonk.[21]

his nonsense is not genuine non-sense. It is a spurious irrationality, the un-reason of a rational mind, obtained by a careful process of inverting both the words within the sentence and the letters within the word:

> Wat did need? Knot. Wat ad got? Knot. Was kup ful? Pah! But did need? Praps not. But ad got? Know not.

REFERENCES

1. *W.*, pp. 28–9.
2. *W.*, p. 38.
3. *W.*, p. 181 (normal order restored).
4. Beckett used to read Mauthner's *Beiträge zu einer Kritik der Sprache* aloud to Joyce (Ellmann, *op. cit.*, p. 661).
5. See Hoefer, "Watt," in *Perspective*, 1959. An important study, from which much of this argument is derived.
6. *W.*, p. 128
7. *W.*, p. 126.
8. *W.*, pp. 88–9.
9. *W.*, pp. 78–9.
10. *W.*, p. 44.
11. *W.*, p. 46.
12. Wittgenstein, *Tractatus*, Proposition 6.54. See Hoefer, *op. cit.*, pp. 180–1.
13. *W.*, p. 48.
14. *All That Fall*, p. 27.
15. *Murphy*, p. 96.
16. Kenner, *op. cit.*, p. 107. Once again, I am heavily indebted to Prof. Kenner's arguments.
17. Kenner, *op. cit.*, p. 105.
18. *Molloy*, p. 112.
19. *W.*, pp. 146–50.
20. *W.*, p. 148.
21. *W.*, p. 182.

CHAPTER IV

THE LONG SONATA OF THE DEAD

Watt, written between 1942 and 1944, while Beckett was in hiding in the Vaucluze, working as a farm-hand, marks the end of his first period of writing in English. The series of novels (*Molloy*, *Malone Dies*, *The Unnamable*) which form the *Trilogy* were all written in French, as was *Waiting for Godot*; but they were not undertaken without a variety of preliminary experiments. Three at least of these experiments proved unsatisfactory, and have remained unpublished: a novel, *Mercier et Camier*; a play, *Eleuthéria*; and a short-story entitled "Premier Amour." This last was probably destined to form the second of a loosely-linked quartet of stories, of which the other three, "L'Expulsé," "Le Calmant," and "La Fin" (written *c*. 1945) were published ten years later, together with the *Textes pour rien*. These three *Nouvelles*, in their desperate search for a "Self," an identity that lies beyond the barrier of words, already foreshadow the main theme of the *Trilogy*, and constitute the link between *Watt* and *Molloy*.

Molloy (written *c*. 1947) falls into two sections, the second being a form of commentary on the first, the rational attempting—and failing—to explain and as it were catch up with the irrational, the infinite. The first part tells of the journey of Molloy in search of his mother. Concerning his departure, we know all the details:

> I resolved to go and see my mother. I needed, before I could resolve to go and see that woman, reasons of an urgent nature, and with such reasons, since I did not

know what to do, or where to go, it was child's play for me, the play of an only child, to fill my mind until it was rid of all other preoccupation and I seized with a trembling at the mere idea of being hindered from going there, I mean to my mother, there and then . . .[1]

but by what means he eventually reaches her, we never discover, although he is in her room already when the story opens. For his journey, which begins on the inevitable bicycle, is interrupted when he runs over a small dog, is arrested, is rescued by the owner of the late animal, "a Mrs Loy, or Lousse"; and the narrative in the end just peters out, leaving Molloy alone in the forest, his bicycle lost and his own body having decayed to the point where he can scarcely crawl, all hope and all desire abandoned: "Molloy could stay, where he happened to be."

If Molloy is the "irrational number," Moran is the integer. To Moran, Molloy's very existence is problematic. "Perhaps I had invented him," he muses, "I mean found him ready-made in my head."[2] Even of the name, "Molloy or Mollose," he is decidedly uncertain—or rather, he is quite certain of the beginning (one *can* be quite certain of the beginning of π), but the end seems strangely difficult to grasp. None the less, Moran— obscurely a cross between a secret agent and a private detective—is ordered by his "Chief," Youdi, to go out in search of Molloy. In spruce and orderly fashion, and accompanied by his son, he sets out; but as soon as he reaches "the Molloy country," his body also begins to decay. He sends his son to buy a bicycle, which in its turn disintegrates, eventually disappears; and so Moran, half staggering, half crawling like Molloy himself, at last reaches home again, his mission unaccomplished.

Between these two parts there is no comparison. Moran remains a contrived and allegorical figure; Molloy from the first transcends his arid intellectual

origins and achieves a rich and unforgettable humanity.
His "I" seems to embrace the whole of human experience
and intellect, the whole of good and evil, poetry and
cruelty, which has been assimilated, discarded, ground
into the dust of a supreme, contemptuous indifference:
"It's a change of muck. And if all muck is the same muck
that doesn't matter, it's good to have a change of muck."[3]
Yet "indifference" is perhaps inaccurate. "All roads were
right for me," he comments, "a wrong road was an event
for me"; yet at the same time, all roads lead to suffering,
life is an intolerable burden to be borne, birth a worse
injustice than death. Suffering is the one incontrovertible
fact of life. It *is* existence, it is the proof that "something
is taking its course," it could even be evidence of the
Self. "Je souffre, donc je suis." "I know my eyes are
open," says The Unnamable, "because of the tears that
pour from them unceasingly."[4] And Vladimir: "The air
is full of our cries." Man is born unto trouble as the
sparks fly upwards—but *why*? There is no reason; the
pain, the disintegration of the human machine are
utterly gratuitous. "What makes me weep so? From time
to time. There is nothing saddening here. Perhaps it is
liquefied brain"—so speaks The Unnamable again. So
intense is Beckett's pity for the gratuitous suffering of
man that at times it seems almost intolerable—it is the
angoisse that runs through all his work. If existence is such
suffering, then it were better not to exist. And so, for
Beckett's people, the unforgivable sin is to love; for the
"music, *music*, MUSIC" which is love is inseparable
from the primeval curse—the Calvinistic original sin—
of sex. "Love" creates new beings to endure suffering;
and, for Molloy, the term "mother" is the obscenest
swear-word in his vocabulary. She is "that blind and
sordid hag," she is the one "who brought me into the
world, through the hole in her arse if my memory is
correct. First taste of the shit."[5] Were it not for birth,
how much suffering might not be spared—how much

absurdity, disaster, futility and death. The decay, the progressive disintegration that Molloy experiences, the whole sordid, malodorous, obscene Calvary-procession from womb to refuse-dump—this is the responsibility of her whom Molloy calls "Mag."

Yet this is only the beginning of the puzzle; for Molloy, having an existence, possesses it only as one member of a series, therefore he is not free. His beginning was determined by another, just as his son's beginning, if he has one, will be determined by him. Molloy hates no one in the world so much as Mag; Moran hates no one so much as his son. Watt's preoccupation with the intolerable determinism of the series is transferred by Molloy into the "chain of generations"—and in addition, Molloy is obsessed with a need for freedom in a way quite foreign to Watt. He feels his freedom threatened on all sides; his very life itself is a sequence of "hypothetical imperatives," and these imperatives, he notes, "nearly all bore on the same question, that of my relations with my mother." He is imprisoned in the chain of life, the three-part sonata-form of beginning-waiting-ending. And there is no escape.

But unlike the sequence of servants in Mr Knott's house, where the arrival of the third automatically determined the departure of the first, the act of progeniture is not in itself an end. Something has gone wrong here in the sequence—time has got out of step with logic, and seems somehow to be protracting itself quite unwarrantably. There seems to be no end. Molloy is already almost as old as his mother, he notes, and his son, if he had one, would be almost as old as himself. Birth is an irrevocable beginning for him who is born; but it is not, as it should be logically, an irrevocable end for her who gives birth or for him who engenders. There seems to be a rigidly determining enslavement at one end of existence, and a sort of indeterminate and timeless freedom at the other. It is as though the arrival of the number 7 were

E

ruthlessly determined by the number 6, but that, having once begun, 7 could continue indefinitely, regardless of the arrival of 8, 9, 10, etc. In any case, whatever death is, it is not merely the corresponding opposite of birth. There is no conceivable way of reconciling the arbitrary determinism of birth with the freedom of him who is born. But it *is* just possible to think of death as freedom.

Of his own essential freedom, Molloy, despite occasional hesitations, has little real doubt. It is the freedom of the Geulincxian "bodytight mind," the freedom of the Void, the *pour-soi*, of the Self which escapes both reason and the senses:

> And once again I am, I will not say alone, no, that's not like me, but, how shall I say, I don't know, restored to myself, no, I never left myself, free, yes, I don't know what that means, but it's the word I mean to use, free to do what, to do nothing, to know, but what, the laws of the mind perhaps, of my mind. . . .[6]

On the other hand, it is freedom within a deterministic framework, the freedom of the slave to crawl east along the deck of a boat travelling west; and the limiting factor is life. If life is infinite, even if only at one end, then freedom is likewise infinite; but if life is limited by the monstrosity of death as well as by that of birth, and if, within that narrow space, every physical action is arranged beforehand in terms of a Malebranchian or Leibnizian "pre-established harmony," what freedom is there? Merely a thinly-veiled compulsion. "We agents," says Moran, "often amused ourselves with giving ourselves the airs of free men."[7] But then Moran, unlike Molloy, is a rational integer, hemmed in on both sides by the series. His ending is of the same nature as his beginning. Whereas Molloy's ending is the unknown factor, *x*.

Thus Beckett's people find themselves inextricably involved in problems of beginning and ending, of birth and especially of death. Beckett's very titles reveal his preoccupations: "La Fin," *Fin de partie*, *La Dernière Bande*, and the punning *Comment c'est* ("commencer"). So also does his style: the form of narrative in *Molloy* spirals repeatedly inward around itself, so that it has no beginning and no end; its end is the writer writing the beginning; its beginning—Molloy inexplicably at home in his mother's room—is in fact its end. It is a continuously expanding present, and at the same time an infinite progression: the writer writing about a past which can never catch up with the present moment of writing, because, even as he writes the word "now," or "it is midnight," the instant of "now" has already vanished, and "it was not midnight."[8] About beginnings, Beckett has little to say which is of immediate importance: we cannot *remember* our beginning, so perhaps it never was. We are forced to rely on hearsay. Of Watt he notes tantalisingly, in the Addenda: "never been properly born," and it is interesting that the same phrase recurs in *All That Fall*. But of this we may be certain, that if there *is* a beginning, then it is arbitrary and abrupt. "L'Expulsé" is literally flung down the steps of his house into the gutter. But endings are a different matter altogether. Even $\pi = 3.14159 \ldots$ begins abruptly enough: but for its ending you may wait and wait till Doomsday ... or "for Godot to come ... or for night to fall."

Thus death becomes the main subject of the *Trilogy*, but not in any ordinary sense. Not one of Beckett's people is afraid of death. Some long for it (Hamm, for instance), but all, without exception, are desperately puzzled about its meaning and its mechanism. All think of life as an exile, a punishment for some unknown crime, perhaps the crime of being born, as Estragon suggests—an exile in time from the reality of themselves, which reality is, and must be, timeless. All think of their essential Self as spatial, yet dimensionless, as "a mote in the dark of absolute freedom" (Murphy), as "a speck in the void, in the dark, for ever" (Hamm), as living out a Belacqua-purgatory before their re-admission to the timelessness of Nothing—but none of them see death itself as really relevant. For either death just simply annihilates—in which case it abolishes the problems of life without solving them; or else life continues indefinitely beyond death, in which case the problems remain unsolved. What is needed to close the exile is an *end*—an end which is a resolution of logical impossibilities and which must therefore be an introduction into a different dimension altogether (the dimension where $\sqrt{2}$ is a rational number), an end which is in the same instant a beginning; and it is extremely improbable that death can offer this. Death itself is a temporal phenomenon, destroying other temporal phenomena—words, memories, bicycles. But how can death destroy, let alone resolve, a Void, a Self? Or time? Or space? Destruction, in fact, is almost as literally inconceivable as survival. There simply are no words: "All I know is what the words know," says Molloy:

and the dead things, and that makes a handsome little sum, with a beginning, a middle and an end, as in the well-built phrase and the long sonata of the dead.[9]

So irrelevant is death, in fact, that Molloy, and Malone after him, are by no means certain that they are not dead already. They cannot recall their birth, so why should they necessarily recall their death? For Beckett's people, the boundary between life and after-life becomes progressively vaguer. Molloy cannot recall whether his mother was dead or not when last he saw her; and of himself, he notes sometimes, with surprise, that he is still alive ("that may come in useful"), at other times that he is dead ("it is only since I ceased to live that I think of these things"), at others again, that both are true at once.

But then, if death is not the end, what is the end? For an end there must be, if this intolerable exile from the

Self, the *Nichts*, is ever to conclude. *Comment finir?* is the tormenting question. For Molloy, the problem is insoluble. For, on the one hand, for anything to begin or end, by Watt's "law of series," implies a rigid determinism before and after, and hence a lack of freedom for the Self, which, being a Void, cannot be anything but free. A "total freedom" made to correspond with the Self is only possible in a world (literally) "without end," *i.e.*, without time. But time is inseparable from movement —therefore this freedom is only conceivable in a world without movement either—a world of motionless *waiting*. Or, to look at the same problem from another angle, if the Self *is* totally free, this means that time and movement are illusions, or perhaps just impossibilities—hence the intolerable difficulty that Beckett's people seem to have in going anywhere, or else the terror with which Molloy observes the beginning or ending of anything:

> From things about to disappear, I turn away in time. To watch them out of sight, no, I can't do it.[10]

To end, therefore, is intolerable, as it immures him for ever in the determinism of the series; and not to end is equally intolerable, for then there is no escape from time. In this *angoisse*, Molloy has two half-comforts. The first is —like the recurring decimal—to envisage an end without ever actually contemplating reaching it. Thus every happening, for Molloy, is "the last but two, perhaps, before the end":

> This time, then once more I think, then perhaps a last time, then I think it'll be over. . . .[11]

The second is an expedient, apparently harmless, but full of consequences for Molloy's successors, which consists in reliving, after an interval of time, an event already once lived through, in such a way that the two experiences merge, and in merging, annihilate the interval of time which separated them. For Molloy, the *unique* experience is unbearable; but reiterated experiences superimposed one on top of the other may create an apparently single, yet in fact compound experience, from which the element of time has been abstracted. And as his memory decays and his personality disintegrates, so he includes in his reiterations, experiences which perhaps belonged to other people. Thus step by step he builds up—by the old Belacqua-process of reliving experiences once lived already—an odd, provisional existence outside time, a Self which merges with the Selves of others as the first step on the road to the ultimate Self which merges with the Nothing.

At the outset of the second novel of the *Trilogy* (*Malone Dies*, written *c.* 1948), Malone has already attained to that state which Molloy reaches only at the conclusion of his pilgrimage: he is static, motionless, in bed and dying —but less easily persuaded that he is already dead. For certain ideas which Molloy no more than touched upon, are here allowed a much broader development. For Malone, the act of dying is not nearly so irrelevant in itself as it was for Molloy, since, to begin with, the physical death entails suffering, and in the fact of suffering, Malone sees a glimmering of hope that he may realise or grasp his own identity. It is the basically gratuitous character of suffering which intrigues him, the fact that the apparent "causes" of any particular pain or misery in no way suffice to explain or justify the experience ("as if there existed a relationship between that which suffers and that which causes to suffer," he exclaims);[12] suffering, therefore, escapes the laws of cause and effect, it springs from the uncaused Void, and consequently belongs to the same order of being as the Self, and may be actual, verifiable evidence of its reality. If this were so, then Malone would welcome nothing more eagerly than suffering—would even willingly inflict it on himself, as does Macmann's "keeper," Lemuel, with his hammer. But the trouble is that the most vivid "evidence" of suffering is *physical*, consequently is temporal and irrelevant: "How bearable all that is, my God!" Reluctantly, therefore, he consents to abandon his attempt to reach his inner being directly through the consciousness of pain—not that he abandons it entirely, but rather he puts forward an alternative hypothesis. Suffering, admittedly, is causeless and gratuitous in itself: but maybe its effect works backwards, maybe, like the end-term of a series, it does in fact, by its existence, create and determine a preceding cause. It is the "atonement" for a "sin": but the "sin" is not the cause of the "atonement," rather the fact of the atonement creates the logical necessity of the sin. What that sin is, Malone has no idea:

> And without knowing exactly what his sin was he felt full well that living was not a sufficient atonement for it or that this atonement was in itself a sin, calling for more atonement, and so on, as if there could be anything but life, for the living.[13]

—none the less, the irrational factor of suffering is at least evidence of the existence of something else irrational—if not of a Self beyond the grasp of reason, at least of an irrational order of things, of which the Self may be one part, and the "sin" another. Life is not an end in itself; life exists in order that suffering may exist, and that thus the Self may keep contact with, perhaps eventually rejoin, the causeless, timeless Totality to which it truly belongs. Clov, in *Endgame*, has the same idea:

> I say to myself—sometimes, Clov, you must learn to suffer better than that if you want them to weary of punishing you—one day. I say to myself—sometimes, Clov, you must be there better than that if you want them to let you go—one day.[14]

Malone, then, is far more aware than Molloy of the

actual mechanism of death in relation to the Self. But he is different also in that he is far more deeply conscious of the unbridgeable gap between his "pseudo-Self" (as "Malone") and his unfathomable reality. Molloy only very occasionally thinks of his "I" as something other than simply "Molloy." Like the ideal Cartesian man, he "thinks continuously"; if he ceased to think, he would cease to be. But since "thoughts," as Wittgenstein has shown, have no existence unless in words, Molloy (quite literally) *speaks* continuously, in one immense, unpausing monologue; for if his words dried up, he, as "Molloy," would no longer exist. What would then remain, he dare not contemplate, for, to do so, he would have to stop talking and plunge into the *Néant*. He is aware of the essential unreality of his pseudo-Self, compounded out of words, yet not strong enough to analyse it—he is blinded, as it were, by the very unity of his own "personality"; his "moi" is either "Molloy," or nothing.

Not so Malone. Malone *is* able to analyse those factors (thoughts, words, memories) which make up the "over-coat" of personality and hide his real Self, and he understands that, out of other thoughts, words, memories, all equally arbitrary, he can create a whole series of different "personalities," none of which is either more or less real than "Malone." Where there is one "Molloy," there can be two or three "Malones" (to whom, for convenience' sake, he gives different names: Malone . . . Saposcat . . . Macmann), each in an identical relationship to the inner Void which is his Self. Thus his "I," as narrator, stands at a distance from himself in whatever provisional incarnation, and can observe with more detachment; he is not irrevocably committed to being "Malone," as Molloy was to being "Molloy." And *if*—and this is his ultimate intention—he can make the death of one of his pseudo-personalities (in the event, Macmann) correspond exactly with the death of his more permanent pseudo-personality, "Malone," then perhaps his "I" may be able to stand aside from both, and so observe the mechanism of death in time, and possibly (who knows?) in that instantaneous-infinite moment of crisis, grasp at or penetrate the *Néant* of the timeless Self.

Thus Malone, as he lies in bed, motionless, in his "room," which may be some sort of poor-house, or may equally well, like Hamm's, be the inside of his own head, hooking occasionally at his few possessions which lie hidden in the darker corners (the subconscious?) with his stick (memory? consciousness?), achieves the almost perfect *stasis* of Beckettian man. And as he waits for death, he "tells himself stories," of Macmann, of Saposcat:

> While waiting I shall tell myself stories, if I can. They will not be the same kind of stories as hitherto, that is all. They will be neither beautiful nor ugly, they will be calm, there will be no ugliness or beauty or fever in them any more, they will be almost lifeless, like the teller. What was that I said? It does not matter. I look forward to their giving me great satisfaction, some satisfaction. I am satisfied, there. . . .[15]

Malone's first "story" fails, for the simple reason that he soon grows bored with his own hero, Saposcat. "What tedium," he interrupts repeatedly, "mortal tedium." With his second try, however, he is more successful. Macmann is another of Beckett's inimitable vagabonds, half-way, perhaps, between Molloy and Estragon. But the final question, whether Malone's stratagem to escape from time by reduplicating his own pseudo-personalities —his careful plan to "die alive"—in fact succeeds, is still left open as the novel finishes. Malone himself is tortured by doubt. For somehow, he can never lose himself wholly in his alternative identities; continually he is dragged back into himself, Malone, and this "Malone," alone of all his incarnations, appears inextricably plunged in life. Life, and therefore time, sticks to it like a burr. Saposcat can just evaporate; Malone must *die*:

> For my stories are all in vain, deep down I never doubted, even the days abounding in proof to the contrary, that I was still alive and breathing in and out the air of the earth.[16]

Or is it so? Malone loses consciousness (his stick, his pencil), regains it, loses it again, gropes progressively towards the Nothing; yet in the end it is Macmann who plunges into the Void:

> never there he will never
> never anything
> there
> any more[17]

—Malone himself is absent. The detached "I" that can observe Macmann perhaps in that same instant can observe Malone . . . and so watch itself die. And if this is the case, if both Macmann and Malone are dead, where is the "I," *what* is the "I" that can survive and watch its body's death? And where and what, moreover, is that Self, which, being timeless, formless and dimensionless, must be immune to death? These are questions which The Unnamable will have to answer.

Meanwhile, Malone has another problem of his own. He observes (and he is the first of Beckett's people to do so) that the nearer he gets to what must be "the end," the slower time—*his* time—proceeds. In fact, the passage of days and nights becomes irrelevant. He notices it first in the behaviour of the light, which "is bizarre." Dawn leads straight to dusk, without an intervening space of day. "The language of the days" has grown meaningless. Time, in fact, for Malone, as he proceeds towards zero, protracts itself, once again like a recurring decimal, in the direction of infinity, approaching nearer and nearer by increasingly insignificant degrees, yet never attaining its object. And like his predecessors, but with a deeper horror, Malone comes gradually to understand that time, while time is, has no end; and he, in time, has no end either. His death, his real death, which is at the same time a rebirth, will never come. Suddenly he realises that "he feels so far from the morrow":

> And perhaps there is none, no morrow any more, for one who has waited so long for it in vain.[18]

And so he understands, "with a glow of that old frenzy," that he must *kill time*—annihilate it once and for all, destroy the net which holds him for ever, like Tantalus, so near and yet so far—and so he kills: he metaphysically goes berserk. His "stories," in the current sense, are made "to kill the time." He kills the living, for the living live in time:

> The living. They were always more than I could bear, all, no, I don't mean that, but groaning with tedium I watched them come and go, then I killed them, or took their place, or fled . . .[19]

—or else, he breeds such a stillness deep within himself that time has no more meaning—time stops, in fact, for him and for the world. "I stop everything and wait. . . . The turmoil of the day freezes into a thousand absurd postures." Yet nothing works. Time will not stop. It will slow down—it *has* slowed down, so that its motion has ceased to be perceptible—but still it will not die. Time will not die, nor therefore can Malone: his "death" will never be a "real" death, an end, until time itself has ceased. And that will never be. Beginnings there are, and journeys, but no neat ends. There is no end. There is only a waiting, and

> he who has waited long enough will wait for ever. And there comes the hour when nothing more can happen and nobody more can come and all is ended but the waiting that knows itself in vain. . . .[20]

Not a waiting for death, but literally a waiting for Nothing. Beyond death, there is not "Nothing," but simply more waiting. The purgatory of earth is merely transformed into another, of stranger and sadder dimensions—the purgatory of *The Unnamable*.

REFERENCES

1. *Molloy*, p. 16.
2. *Op. cit.*, p. 112.
3. *Op. cit.*, p. 41.
4. *The Unnamable*, p. 306.
5. *Molloy*, p. 16.
6. *Op. cit.*, p. 13.
7. *Op. cit.*, p. 95.
8. *Op. cit.*, cp. pp. 92 and 176.
9. *Op. cit.*, pp. 31-2.
10. *Op. cit.*, p. 12.
11. *Op. cit.*, p. 8.
12. *M.D.*, p. 243.
13. *M.D.*, p. 240.
14. *E.*, p. 51.
15. *M.D.*, p. 180.
16. *M.D.*, p. 234.
17. *M.D.*, p. 289.
18. *M.D.*, p. 233.
19. *M.D.*, p. 194.
20. *M.D.*, p. 242.

CHAPTER V

THE RIGHT KIND OF SILENCE

The dramatic crisis in the *Trilogy* occurs in the blank space between *Malone Dies* and *The Unnamable* (written *c.* 1949); for in that space, Malone-Macmann *does* die ("never anything / there / any more"), and his death solves precisely nothing. Death is not the annihilation of the problem; the problem still persists, if anything in a form still more acute, for now it cannot be evaded any longer, now there are no distractions, no bicycles, no sucking-stones, none of the sordidness and suffering which is life to stand between the "I" and its increasingly anguished questions: "Where now? Who now? When now? Unquestioning. I, say I. Unbelieving." The "I," not merely detached now, but finally and absolutely separated from its pseudo-Selves (its "vice-existers") has no other occupation but to seek its absolute, its void, and so eventually to find its end.

The Unnamable is one of the profoundest explorations of the problem of self-knowledge ever attempted; and if it fails, it is because it must necessarily fail. Knowledge, which is the province of the "I," of consciousness, is positive and finite; the Self, in Beckett's view, is infinite and void. Therefore the one can never grasp the other, save in the act of its own annihilation. But a knowledge which annihilates itself is no longer knowledge, a word which is silence is no longer a word, no longer a thought. The objective, therefore, is literally impossible—yet must be achieved, for to continue for ever reduced to the dimensions of a single question which cannot be answered is a state too agonising to endure. The question *must* be answered, the question *cannot* be answered—and so the book concludes:

> . . . I don't know, I'll never know, in the silence you don't know, you must go on, I can't go on, I'll go on.[1]

In between this beginning and this end (these concepts, of course, have no significance, save in terms of print on the page), the "I" takes stock of its condition in the anti-universe in which it finds itself, and then performs a series of experiments with words and "vice-existers," each one of which promises to bring it a fraction nearer to its goal, the inconceivable centre of the circle, and each one of which, by definition, fails.

But first, The Unnamable must analyse the logical implications of his own survival. In "eternity" (infinite time, timelessness) there can be no end and no beginning, there can be no movement, there can be no thought (since thoughts are words, and words exist only in duration, in time), no memory, no personality. No "I." And yet the "I" exists, or seems to. The Unnamable dimly feels himself to have a physical form ("the shape, if not the consistency, of an egg");[2] but he *knows* that he thinks . . . he thinks, and therefore he is. He is "in words, made of words, others' words. . . ."[3] He is therefore a temporal phenomenon existing in an a-temporal state—he is an anomaly, a logical contradiction which admits of only one resolution: he must conclude that "timelessness" is in fact time which moves in circles. "Eternity" can only be conceived as finite sequences of time infinitely repeated. Moreover, if time in relation to eternity is cyclical, then the same is necessarily true of space. The "I" can survive death only by moving into an Einsteinian fourth dimension.

This awareness of the cyclical nature of time in eternity is the first major experience of The Unnamable. Malone, for instance, his previous "vice-exister," appears before him exactly like a planet before a fixed telescope: "he passes before me at regular intervals . . . he passes close by me, a few feet away, always in the same direction." Malone, somehow, seems to move in a flat orbit; perhaps this is evidence of his essential unreality, for The Unnamable feels that his own movement is more complex: "I must have got embroiled in a kind of spiral," he muses —a spiral leading one way to a dead end, the other extended "ad infinitum . . . or is it the earth?"—and this is also the experience of his first new pseudo-Self, one Basil, later renamed Mahood, who finds himself returning from "a world tour, perhaps," in ever-decreasing spirals about the earth (time slowing up meanwhile, as with Malone, as he approaches the centre), eventually reaching his house to find all his family dead of ptomaine poisoning— whereupon, having stamped hard on the remains, he sets off once again in the reverse direction:

> When I penetrate into that house, if I ever do, it will be to go on turning, faster and faster, more and more convulsive, like a constipated dog, or one suffering from worms, overturning the furniture, in the midst of my family all trying to embrace me at once, until by virtue of a supreme spasm I am catapulted in the opposite direction and gradually leave backwards. . . .[4]

The most interesting characteristic of these new "stories" that The Unnamable tells about himself, is that the border-line between the "I" and the pseudo-Selves has grown almost imperceptible. Malone referred to Macmann as "he." The Unnamable alludes to Mahood as "I," and the various "I"s of his narrative merge into one another so completely, that it is often impossible to tell where one begins, the other ends. Here again, The Unnamable is grappling with the insoluble problem of language. Just as the "I" of the *Nouvelles* felt he might conceivably grasp his ultimate Self if he could devise a non-existent tense to locate himself in time, so The Unnamable is searching for a pronoun. On the one hand, his "I" proliferates into innumerable incarnations; on the other, between the "I" and "he" there is inextricable confusion:

> it is not he, it's I, or another, or others, what does it matter, the case is clear, it is not he, he who I know I am, that's all I know, who I cannot say I am, I can't say anything, I've tried. . . .[5]

At a later stage still, the "I" dissolves into "you" and "they" and "we"—all failures, all equally inadequate to designate the void:

> someone says you, it's the fault of the pronouns, there is no name for me, no pronoun for me, all the trouble comes from that. . . .[6]

Molloy made his journey in irregular octagons, Mahood makes his in infinite spirals; Malone comes to rest on the bed in his room, Mahood in a jar outside a restaurant. The final *stasis* of Mahood is one of Beckett's most grotesque inventions:

> For of the great traveller I had been, on my hands and knees in the later stages, then crawling on my belly or rolling on the ground, only the trunk remains (in sorry trim), surmounted by the head with which we are already familiar. . . . Stuck like a sheaf of flowers in a deep jar, its neck flush with my mouth, on the side of a quiet street near the shambles, I am at rest at last.[7]

Mahood with his successive mutilations resumes in one single identity all his predecessors, from Belacqua to Malone: the progressive decay of the senses, so that the Self may be free at last from determinism by sensory impression, the elimination of the physical body, in order that the "I" may ultimately "die alive," the cutting away of the arbitrary features of human existence, in such a way that the living being may become ever more closely identified with the featureless, impersonal Self—

Faith, that's an idea, yet another, mutilate, mutilate, and perhaps some day, fifteen generations hence, you'll succeed in beginning to look like yourself, among the passers-by[8]

—and finally, the slowing-down and eventual elimination of movement, for movement is life-in-time, and life-in-time is exile for the Self. Between the Self, timeless and dimensionless and therefore absolutely motionless, and the living being, which inherits motion in the same instant that it inherits life, there is, again, an unbridgeable gap. Moreover, as soon as physical movement ceases, the movement of words must compensate. Belacqua moves continuously, talks scarcely at all; Mahood, immobilised for ever in his jar, talks all the time. The Self alone escapes, or rather stands outside, this tyrannical régime of motion, time and thought. Hence its dilemma. It dare not think about itself, and yet to know itself, it cannot help but think. To think, to be, to be even in thought, is to give the initial impulse to that motion which, hence-forward, can never be brought to rest. Thus for the Self to think about the Self is to destroy itself. It can, as always, be defined only in terms of what it is not. It is not "I"—it therefore is "not-I." And so The Unnamable proceeds to the last and most extraordinary of his incarnations, the incarnation of an Absolute Negative, to which, for want of better, he gives the name of Worm.

If I have hesitated from the start to insist upon any mystic interpretation of Beckett's doctrine of the Void, it is because other, more rationalist philosophies have reached identical conclusions without the need to entangle themselves in the minor absurdities of the Tao and Za-Zen. Of these, the most significant by far is Existentialism, and in particular that part of Sartrian philosophy which postulates the *Néant* of the Self. Beckett's relationships with Existentialism as such are complex and hard to define. With *Murphy*, he revealed himself an *existentialiste*

F

avant la lettre; yet ostensibly he has always kept clear of the movement, always denied any form of affiliation. Many of his people—Molloy, Malone, for instance—seem to be Existentialists who have failed, who have quite literally collapsed beneath the burdens of choice, responsibility and *angoisse* which Existentialism lays upon the sagging shoulders of the human race. They do not even bother to argue the case for a Sartrian view of the human condition, they take it for granted, it does not need to be proved to them. In *The Unnamable*, however, the case is different. Not that The Unnamable himself is either more or less of a crypto-Existentialist than his predecessors; he does, however, take two specific concepts out of *L'Etre et le Néant* and applies them and their consequences to himself. And these two concepts are those of *le Pour-soi* and of *l'Autre*.

Neither Sartre nor Beckett is prepared to argue about the "real existence" of the material world. Sartre proves it somewhat sketchily, and then hurries on to his main problem, which is man's relation to it. For him, as for the Buddhist, that which exists, exists as an undifferentiated mass, a "fullness," until it becomes the object of perception. Only a mind can distinguish between, say, a table and a chair, an inch and a mile, red and yellow, and it does so by applying negatives. It determines "yellow" by eliminating all the colours that are *not* yellow. Only the mind can say "Peter is not there"—in a "massive," undifferentiated universe, the statement is an absurdity. "Absence" is a mental concept, not a fact. There are no negatives in nature.

Consciousness, therefore, is the imposing of a negative on a positive—a process of "néantisation." It follows that the cosmos is of a dual character: all that massively exists ("l'être" or "l'en-soi") is positive, while consciousness, which organises that which exists, is negative ("le néant," or "le pour-soi"). Logically therefore, the *pour-soi* (the negation which is consciousness) must lie outside all being; only that "which is not" is able to understand that which is. The *pour-soi* is not Being; the *pour-soi* "is its own Not-Being."[9]

And, being negative, the Sartrian *pour-soi* has all the attributes of the Beckettian "Self." It escapes the causal order of the world. It is free—so totally free that no static definition of itself is possible. On the other hand, it can invent and re-invent its own "reality" continuously—it "tells itself stories" about its reality, and these stories supply the place of its existence. It is not determined by its own stories—it cannot be determined by anything— and yet it may come to resent them, for they are not itself: they are the "not-I" disguising itself as "I," they are an imposture. Again, being Nothing, it can impose itself on anything; its total freedom is an *angoisse* of hesitation before an infinity of possibilities—or permutations. It cannot be sincere; it cannot say with certain self-knowledge, "I am this" or "I am that," because, being Nothing, it cannot define itself; as soon as it does define itself, it becomes an *en-soi*, an object—it tells a lie. ("It's a lie," says The Unnamable repeatedly.) And finally, the *pour-soi* is impersonal; it abstracts the *ego* from the *cogito*. It borrows its illusion of personality from the memory of experience. The consciousness that defines the world is a consciousness without a subject.

But in this context, what about the Other, whose essential self, like mine, is a negative? He is an object in my world, and yet he makes me an object in his; he is "the hole in my world . . . through which my world escapes." I am infinite, he locates me in time and space, he pins me down. I am his slave. I am a means to his end, I prove to him (by being other than he) that he exists. The Other (*l'Autre*), therefore, is a thing of terror in the Sartrian universe, the tyrant who reduces the eternity and infinity of my own *pour-soi* to the limits of the material object. "L'Enfer, c'est les autres."

And so to Worm. Worm is Beckett's most far-reaching

attempt to incarnate conceptually the *Néant* of the Self—the Sartrian *pour-soi*. Worm is not-Mahood; he is the "anti-Mahood." He *is*, and yet he is Nothing:

> Worm, to say he does not know what he is, where he is, what is happening, is to underestimate him. What he does not know is that there is anything to know. His senses tell him nothing, nothing about himself, nothing about the rest, and this distinction is beyond him. Feeling nothing, knowing nothing, he exists nevertheless, but not for himself, for others, others conceive him and say, Worm is, since we conceive him. . . .[10]

He is pure existence, with none of the arbitrary attribute of life or personality, he

> has nothing, is nothing. Come into the world unborn, abiding there unliving, with no hope of death. . . . The one outside of life we always were in the end, all our long vain life long. . . . The one ignorant of himself and silent, ignorant of his silence and silent, who could not be and gave up trying.[11]

The fact, however, that Mahood can conceive, negatively, the existence of Worm, still does not solve the problem. If he is to achieve his ultimate quietus, he must *become* Worm. But precisely because he is Mahood—that is, conscious and sentient—he cannot become Worm: on the contrary, his very failure to become a Nothing emphasises and as it were "proves" the positive quality of his own "existence" and its falseness. He is not really Mahood (Mahood is an illusion, a pseudo-Self); yet, because he is Mahood, he cannot become what he really is . . . Worm:

> since I couldn't be Mahood, as I might have been, I must be Worm, as I cannot be . . . when I have failed to be Worm I'll be Mahood, automatically, on the rebound. . . .[12]

The alternative, since Mahood cannot resolve himself into Worm, is for Worm to reach out, as it were, towards Mahood. If the *en-soi* cannot identify itself with the *pour-soi*, it is at least conceivable that the *pour-soi*, since it has a real existence, albeit negative, might be able to deck itself out with sufficient conceptual attributes to give it something in common with the *en-soi*. If Worm had but one single element of consciousness, one sense, the sense of hearing, say, if Worm could have one thought, employ one word, he could communicate with Mahood, who is all words, he could throw a single thread across the abyss which Mahood could grasp. The idea is at least worth trying. And so Beckett reverses his usual procedure, which is progressively to eliminate the senses of his "people" so that they may approximate to Worm, and, borrowing Condillac's image of a statue endowed with the different senses one by one ("They mentioned roses. I'll smell them before I'm finished"),[13] tentatively allows his Worm to hear. Joyfully, Mahood grasps at the thread, glimpses at last a possibility of becoming Worm: "Quick, a place. With no way in, no way out, a safe place. Not like Eden. And Worm inside."—only to realise in the same instant that a Worm who hears is no longer Worm, but is merely a projection of himself. The Nothing that conceives itself is not a Nothing. "I'm Worm, that is to say I am no longer he, since I hear." The last experiment has failed.

And yet The Unnamable still struggles on. He has been defeated by the Word—the word without which no thought, no awareness is conceivable, and yet which does not belong to the Self, but only to the Others—to Mahood, Malone, Macmann, Molloy, to all his "vice-existers," but never to himself. To Beckett, quite literally, as to Sartre, "Hell is other people." For we do not make our words—we learn them. From others. Others speak and we hear. Not a thought in our heads, not a memory, not a fragment of our personality, which was not arbitrarily created and put there by other people.

Beckett extends Sartre's concept of the Other to include not only personalities distinct from "myself," but my own "I" in all its various manifestations. "I," as I conceive myself to be, am already an Other in relation to the essential *Néant*—inevitably so, since the very concept "I" is made up of words learnt from outside. Thus The Unnamable, in absolute despair, comes to realise that even his notion of Worm, of Nothingness, is infinitely far removed from the reality of his Self, since the very word and concept "Nothing" could not exist, were it not for the Others. "Nothing" is a word "they" say. And with this realisation, "they" begin to intrude more and more threateningly into the narrative. The Unnamable feels himself surrounded by a sort of hostile and contemptuous committee, made up of "them":

> all is a question of voices, I say what I am told to say, in the hope that some day they will weary of talking at me. The trouble is I say it wrong, having no ear, no head, no memory. Now I seem to hear them say it is Worm's voice beginning, I pass on the news, for what it is worth. Do they believe I believe it is I who am speaking? That's theirs too. To make me believe I have an ego all my own, and can speak of it, as they of theirs. Another trap to snap me up among the living.[14]

This problem of an apparently coherent "I," which in fact is brought into existence entirely by the tyrannical presence of "voices" from the outside, has preoccupied Beckett ever since *Watt*, who "heard nothing [of] Mr Spiro's conversation, because of other voices, singing, crying, stating, murmuring, things unintelligible in his ear." The Unnamable, in a last despairing effort, undertakes to defeat "them" with their own irresistible weapon —words. Words are all he has. But words are rational, words exist in time; if he can defeat or destroy the rationality of words, pour them out in a massive and torrential jumble defying time and structure, detach them from their contexts, flood the world, the universe, with words, then there is a chance—a remote and unimaginable chance, but never mind—either that by some fluke, one in a million million, he may hit upon that inconceivable combination which will define himself, or else that, being made of words himself, these words, as though by some chemical process or a passage through fire, may coalesce into a new substance, a new reality of himself; or finally, that in the interstices of language used as never it was intended, there may appear the first traces of that new and inexistent language for which all Beckett's people have been seeking: the unutterable, unuttered language of the "I" that can attain the Self. Perhaps the stratagem succeeds, for in the final pages, "they" retreat. But we shall never know. For the ultimate language of the Self is silence, and in silence the *Trilogy* ends. But is it the "right kind" of silence—the silence of Nirvana, or the silence of exhaustion? "For it is all very fine to keep silence, but one has also to consider the kind of silence one keeps."[15] The question is unanswered.

Between the conclusion of the *Trilogy* and the appearance of *Comment c'est* in 1961, Beckett seems to have abandoned the novel as a literary form. Only fragments have survived from this period—the thirteen curious meditations, almost prose-poems, collected under the title *Textes pour rien* (written in 1950), and the opening pages of another novel, discarded and finally transformed into a monologue for broadcasting which was first heard in 1957 under the title *From an abandoned Work*. The latter is of no great significance; The *Textes pour rien*, however, include some of the profoundest and most difficult passages that Beckett has written, and, unless read in the context of the *Trilogy*, may seem well-nigh impenetrable.

While the essential themes remain the same as those of *The Unnamable*, there is a distant shift of focus which has the effect of clarifying the various stages of the disintegration of the human personality. This change is brought about by the development of two specific images: that of the "underground man" (possibly borrowed from Dostoevsky) and that of the "courtroom," with its overtones of Kafka. In *The Unnamable*, the "Self," the "I," the "pseudo-Selves," and the "Others" all seemed to move more or less in the same dimensionless void; but from *Texte ii* onwards, the essential Self and the I-narrator together have moved downwards, into an "underground region" of perpetual darkness, while the Others now inhabit a world of light above. This new image enables Beckett to see the relationships more clearly. The "I" is now a sort of brooding, subterranean *angoisse*, unborn, undying, which sends "up there into the light" a series of pseudo-Selves to live their various lives, and to bring back to it the information which constitutes its knowledge. In contrast to these "vice-existers," the Self possesses at least a relative immortality; but it remains a void, impersonal and ignorant. The "information" it possesses never relates to itself, but only to its representatives. Consequently the problem of "proving" its own reality grows ever more urgent.

This need for evidence forms the second main theme of the *Textes*. The "I," composed of others' words, has no evidence of its identity unless it is "witnessed"; the essential Self, a void, has no proof that it exists save in the existence of some other being sprung from it. The primary need, then, is to witness and be witnessed. Even Mr Knott needs to be witnessed, which is why he keep his servants. Likewise Mahood exists to "testify to" the existence of the Unnamable. Where all the reality of the Self is a *Néant*, to prove the positive existence of that *Néant* is a categorical imperative of life. Otherwise, why live? The "I" of the *Textes* is the first to ask this question, the first also, in a strange way, to try to answer it. He (the narrator) is the Recording Clerk at a trial (*Texte v*—in a courtroom where the very fact of existence is being questioned. His written word is proof—*he* writes, but the word remains, the word alone exists outside the "I":

Je tiens le greffe, je tiens la plume, aux audiences de je ne sais quelle cause. Pourquoi vouloir que ce soit la mienne, je n'y tiens pas. Voilà que ça reprend, voilà la première question de ce soir. Être juge et partie, témoin et avocat, et celui, attentif, indifférent, qui tient le greffe.[16]

This theme—the need for something, someone—to bear witness to the Self, recurs again and again in Beckett's work. In *Comment c'est* it dominates the latter part: it is the "I" of consciousness observing and recording both the *Néant* of the Self and the absurd activities of the pseudo-Self. But it is also the need for others, even the need for God, Beckett's people are solitaries; their "conversations" are absurdities, their egos express themselves only in monstrous monologues; they loathe, detest and fear the Other—and yet they cannot do without the Other, they need him, for, without him as a witness, they cannot know that they exist themselves. This is the secret of the relationship between the "pairs" in Beckett's world—between Hamm and Clov, Pozzo and Lucky, between Bom and Pim, or most characteristically between Vladimir and Estragon. There is no *a priori* basis of friendship between the two tramps; they are constantly wondering if they would not do better to part. But, quite literally, they need each other in order to exist—to *prove* their own identities. "You did see us, didn't you?" asks Vladimir anxiously of the Boy. But next day the Boy has forgotten. So has Pozzo. Only Estragon testifies to Vladimir; only Vladimir bears witness to Estragon . . .

And Mr Knott, needing nothing if not, one, not to need, and, two, a witness to his not needing, of himself knew nothing. And so he needed to be witnessed. Not that he might know, no, but so that he might not cease.[17]

From the "I" which bears witness to the essential Self to the "I" which needs the Other to testify to its own existence, and out of this need breeds a relationship which might—almost—give a reality to friendship and make something other than a clownish farce of love—such is the development of Beckett's later work, from *Godot* and the *Textes* to *Happy Days* and *Comment c'est*.

Comment c'est, however, is one of the strangest and most original novels of our time. By contrast to *The Unnamable*, which seeks to overwhelm the rationalistic limitations of language in an unquenchable torrent of words, *Comment c'est* goes to the opposite extreme and, discarding syntax and punctuation alike, reduces language to its most arid and skeletal form—a limited number of fleshless and colourless phrases which recur time and time again in slightly varied contexts, and which are grouped together in semi-isolated "blocks" of meaning, each one of which has the density, say, of a chapter of *The Brothers Karamazov* quintessentially reduced to the dimensions of a telegram. Nothing remains of "literature" in the traditional sense, save the bare minimum of utterance necessary to convey the essence of an act, of a situation. If the language of *The Unnamable* has something of the Niagara Falls quality of the later Joyce, that of *Comment c'est* has the classic asceticism of a Racine. By reducing language to its barest minimum, by killing the individual life of words and making them the abject slaves of the situation they are ordered to describe, perhaps the tyranny of the Other may be thwarted; perhaps, through their very sparseness, it may be possible to glimpse the wordless reality which lies beneath.

The situation of the "I" of *Comment c'est* is simply that of The Unnamable who has failed—and knows that he has failed—to escape from time into the *Néant*. He has evaded time as a continuum, only to fall into time as a series of cycles. He has achieved his instantaneity, but at a cost. Or rather, all time, past, present and future, has

resolved itself into an instantaneous present ("il crie
toujours je suis fixé je le répète ça ne marche pas au passé
non plus je n'aurai jamais de passé jamais eu",[18]) because
past, present and future are cyclical, and every series of
acts in time repeats itself to infinity. All past, all future
(for future is merely past repeated) exist simultaneously,
but in the form of disconnected fragments of present
consciousness: each "block" of words, in fact, is a
fragment of time extracted from eternity, realised provisionally in the present in one of its infinite repetitions:

> l'énorme passé même récent même lointain des très
> vieux le vieil aujourd'hui ou encore l'oiseau-mouche
> dit l'instant qui passe tout ça
> l'énorme passé oiseau-mouche il vient de gauche on
> le suit des yeux vif demi-cercle destrorsum puis répit
> puis le suivant puis puis ou on les ferme préférable . . .[19]

The present "I," however, unlike The Unnamable,
feels little of the anguish of resentment and futility which
had tormented his predecessor. He is no longer tortured
by hope. The situation of the finite in infinity is anoma-
lous, absurd, impossible: Godot has come, and nothing
essential has been changed. He is the "underground
man" now, for ever; and as he crawls through the mud
and the eternal darkness:

> dix mètres quinze mètres demi-flanc gauche pied
> droit main droite pousse tire plat ventre éjaculations
> muettes demi-flanc droit pied gauche main gauche
> pousse tire plat ventre éjaculations muettes pas un iota
> à changer à cette description[20]

on a journey whose object (contact with one Pim) he
vaguely visualises and vaguely longs for, he considers his
being with a kind of resignation which is new in Beckett's
people. He is still Belacqua, but

> Belacqua basculé sur le côté las d'attendre oublié
> des coeurs où vit la grâce endormie[21]

—a Belacqua who knows that his purgatory will have no end; and having abandoned all hope, save that of reaching Pim, he begins to savour his very indifference, to derive from infinitesimally small variations of comfort and discomfort within the unbroken circle of infinite futility, a kind of happiness. He has his "pictures" of an alien life "up there in the light"; he has his food (tinned sardines, in a symbolic "sack"); he has, or has had, or will have, Pim:

> de bons moments bons pour moi on parle de moi pour lui aussi on parle de lui aussi heureux aussi à sa façon je le saurai plus tard je saurai de quelle façon son bonheur je l'aurai je n'ai pas encore tout eu[22]

"Another happy day," says Winnie later, in the same half-anguished, half-ironic tone. For the current "I," although there is no escape from eternity, no death, no end, no promise of silence any more, there are consolations, and the greatest of these is Pim. Pim is the promise of human contact, of a need satisfied, of communication, of companionship. And as the crawling, nauseating journey continues, Pim seems a haven, a beacon of hope in an eternal void of hopelessness, a goal: the goal of communication.

The encounter with Pim, when it actually occurs, is painful beyond description—one of the most savage and bitter caricatures of human "love" or friendship that has ever been written, Naked, spreadeagled in the filth and darkness, these two beings lie beside each other and "communicate." "I" cannot talk; Pim can, theoretically, but has forgotten the art, and must be reminded—*is* reminded by having a tin-opener jabbed ferociously into his rump, nails dug into his armpits, the handle of the tin-opener jabbed into the small of his back until he howls with pain, But gradually, by infinitely small degrees (and Beckett describes each stage with scientific accuracy), the cries of pain develop into language:

hé vous moi quoi je ne hé vous moi quoi je ne ça va ça
va j'ai compris . . .[23]

and communication is possible; but meanwhile the
dream of love ("un jour nous reprendons la route en-
semble . . .") has degenerated into the Sartrian reality:
lover and beloved are tyrant and slave, executioner and
victim. The narrator asks his questions by scoring letters
in the flesh of Pim's back with sadistic frenzy:

j'aurais pu les enfoncer si j'avais voulu j'en avais
envie tirer creuser des sillons profonds boire les hurlements le bleu l'ombre violente . . .[24]

and even so, the subjects of conversation are rapidly
exhausted. Pim whinges, and his misery arouses only
contempt and loathing in his torturer, who sums up in
one unforgettable imprecation the ultimate nausea of
love: "sales larmes d'increvable frère." And then, without warning, Pim has vanished.

The final section of the novel, "comment c'était après
Pim comment c'est," develops the simple narrative of the
journey, the encounter and the bereavement, into a
grotesque apocalyptic vision, in which the various
elements of Beckett's thought—time, logic, permutations,
Karma, infinity—are juggled together in a kaleidoscopic
pattern of despair. For Pim, when he left the "I" (provisionally named Bom), has journeyed onward to meet
another, and to torture him; whereas Bom now lies
abandoned to await the coming of a fourth, this time to
love, be tortured, speak, move on . . . and catch up Pim.
And so the sequence will repeat, in groups of four, *ad
infinitum*, a chain including all humanity, torturers and
tortured, stretching endlessly into the void, not in a circle
this time, but in a straight line having neither beginning
nor end, a *nec plus ultra* of logical futility. This is the
"Tom, Dick and Harry" sequence of *Watt* taken to its
final conclusion. For if, in order to have evidence of our

existence and identity, we need to be "witnessed," then we need communication with the Other. But the Other, as Sartre has demonstrated, is our executioner, therefore two beings cannot "witness" reciprocally—I must either be torturer or tortured, I cannot be both simultaneously; each therefore needs, or is needed by, another still—and hence the chain, the "series." But if the series were to end, then one member of it, the last one, would be "unwitnessed"—would not exist, and this would be "unjust." He would never be able

de s'offrir au regard de
de qui
celui qui fournit les sacs
possible
à son regard le spectacle ce serait une injustice[25]

The laws of justice, it seems, decree that the series shall be infinite. Why justice? Because "on est dans la justice je n'ai jamais entendu dire le contraire."[26] Because that same rationalism which is incarnated dialectically in the concept of "logic" is embodied ethically in that of "justice." Logic implies justice, as Voltaire and his contemporaries discovered. Rationalism, therefore, seen as justice, decrees that the series shall be infinite; yet infinity is precisely that which forever eludes the grasp of rationalism, conceived as logic. Again, the impossible paradox, the insoluble contradiction, has been reached. And, having reached this point, the novel, more or less, explodes. The impossible is that which cannot be. And if it cannot be, is it not "a simpler solution" to suppose that it is not? What are all these apocalyptic visions, these journeyings and torturings, these can-openers and sacks, but *words*? And what are words, if not the echoes of an alien voice, an unreality? And so the "I" proceeds to ask itself its final questions:

si tout ça oui si tout ça n'est pas comment dire pas de
réponse si tout ça n'est pas faux oui

tous ces calculs oui explications oui toute l'histoire
d'un bout à l'autre oui complètement faux oui

ça c'est passé autrement oui tout à fait oui mais
comment pas de réponse comment ça s'est passé pas de
réponse qu'est-ce qui s'est passé pas de réponse
QU'EST-CE QUI S'EST PASSÉ hurlements bon[27]

All that has gone before is cancelled out, and the novel
itself becomes that Void, that silence, that absolute zero,
to which all Beckett's thought is tending.

REFERENCES

1. *The Unnamable*, p. 418.
2. *Op. cit.*, p. 307.
3. *Op. cit.*, p. 390.
4. *Op. cit.*, p. 323.
5. *Op. cit.*, p. 405.
6. *Op. cit.*, p. 408.
7. *Op. cit.*, p. 329.
8. *Op. cit.*, p. 317.
9. Sartre, *L'Être et le néant*, Paris (Gallimard) 1948, p. 59.
10. *The Unnamable*, p. 349.
11. *Ibid.*
12. *The Unnamable*, pp. 349–50.
13. *Op. cit.*, p. 352.
14. *Op. cit.*, p. 348.
15. *Op. cit.*, p. 311.
16. *N.T.P.R.*, p. 149.
17. *W.*, p. 223.
18. *C.C.*, p. 67.
19. *C.C.*, p. 125.
20. *C.C.*, p. 49.
21. *C.C.*, p. 29.
22. *C.C.*, p. 63.
23. *C.C.*, p. 85.
24. *C.C.*, pp. 66–7.
25. *C.C.*, p. 150.
26. *C.C.*, p. 150.
27. *C.C.*, p. 174.

CHAPTER VI

A LITTLE HEAP OF MILLET

That Beckett should turn to the drama as a means of expression was, given his preoccupations, almost inevitable. For the spoken word approximates to the ever-renewed instantaneous present much more closely than does the written sentence; and if Beckett's novels are an attempt to "discover a tense" in which past and future alike dissolve into the "now," his plays resolve that problem by their very structure. Technically, the novelist's problem has always been how to give present immediacy to a form which naturally demands the past; the dramatist's, how to include the past in a form which exists essentially in the present. Beckett's plays, from *Godot* to *Happy Days*, are, as it were, running commentaries on his novels; but inevitably, the various aspects of the problem of Time loom larger, while other themes tend to fade into the background.

En attendant Godot was written at the same period as the *Trilogy* (*c.* 1948–9), and the puzzled anguish of Vladimir and Estragon is very close to that which torments Malone. In an earlier version, the play was entitled simply *En Attendant*—"Waiting." In their desolate landscape—"A country road. A tree"—the two tramps, Vladimir and Estragon, are waiting for the end, *an* end, an end of time, a way of ending time. Their world, like that of Malone and Molloy, is one of incommensurables; only the end will give them reality, incontrovertible evidence of their own identity and existence; for the Self, like $\sqrt{2}$, must exist—we *know* it exists—yet it can never be found. Godot is there, at the end of the decimal, the final term in the series which will determine the sense of all the rest—yet Godot will never be found until Time itself has stopped. Didi and Gogo are *almost* there, they have travelled hundreds of figures after the decimal point; the Void of timelessness, where the "instantaneous now" coincides with eternal duration, is almost within their grasp, and each day takes them nearer to it: but just as each successive figure after the decimal is less significant than its predecessor, progressing closer and closer to zero by infinitesimal degrees, yet never getting there, so each day takes them nearer to Godot, yet each day is progressively more insignificant, and at nightfall the "end" still eludes their grasp just as stubbornly as at daybreak: "It's not over. . . . It's only beginning. . . . It's awful."[1]

If the novels are dominated by "old Geulincx, dead young" and the symbolic dreaming stance of Dante's Belacqua, the Grey Eminence of the plays is the Greek philosopher Zeno. To the nineteenth century, the sort of problem that Zeno was trying to solve seemed merely irrelevant, and his arguments, ingenious intellectual exercises; to Beckett, the inventor of the "demonstration" called "Achilles and the Tortoise" seems more significant than Pythagoras. Zeno is concerned to prove by argument—essentially, by the breakdown of common logic beneath the blows of contradiction and impossibility—that all Being is a Unity; and among the many aspects of his philosophy, all of which have a greater or a lesser relevance to Beckett's preoccupations, he is particularly concerned to show that the movements and thoughts of a finite being in space and time are unrelated to, and incompatible with, the "reality" of the Universe, since the essence of reality is infinity. Among his lesser known dialectical demonstrations, he propounds that of the heap of millet. Take any finite quantity of millet, and pour half of it into a heap. Then take half of the remaining quantity, and add that to the heap. Then half the re-

G

maining quantity again ... and so on. In an infinite universe, the heap could be completed; in a finite universe, never, for the nearer it gets to the totality, the slower it increases.

The opening lines of *Endgame* take up the parable, only the little heap of millet has become a little heap of days: "Finished," says Clov:

> it's finished, nearly finished, it must be nearly finished. Grain upon grain, one by one, and one day, suddenly, there's a heap, a little heap, the impossible heap.[2]

In *Happy Days*, the "heap" actually occupies the centre of the stage: the "heap of time" in which Winnie is buried, up to her waist, later up to her neck—the heap which always promises, yet never actually grants, a death, an end. So also in *Godot*. The tramps are caught up in a Zeno-heap of time: time has almost stopped, but not quite. (At one point, Vladimir actually declares that it has, but he is wrong.) The rhythm of time has grown so slow, in fact, that Estragon's memory cannot go back as far as the beginning of the evening ("I'm not a historian"), while Pozzo's watch records not the hours but the years. By contrast, the tree, which moves still in a "normal" rhythm of time, seems to Didi and Gogo to develop at a startling speed. "Yesterday evening it was all bare and black," exclaims Vladimir, "and now it's covered with leaves. ... In a single night. ... In a single night!"

If there is a difference between the two tramps, it is essentially that Estragon is slightly nearer to timelessness than is Vladimir. He is almost (but still not quite) outside time. His memory is useless, because each day, being all but endless, yet so infinitesimally small in content of events, resembles its predecessors so closely ("What did we do? ... do? ... I suppose we blathered") that his existence in time is already verging upon an infinitely ex-

Words = Self

tended present instant. The very concept of "days" is almost a torture to him. By contrast, Pozzo, on his first entry, still moves at a normal pace. He is still at the beginning of his journey, his hamper is still full of provisions. But like Moran in search of Molloy, the finite in search of the incommensurable, as soon as he comes into contact with Didi and Gogo, his rationality disintegrates, he loses his watch, his senses decay, and the *angoisse* of time overwhelms him. In the time taken since "yesterday"—the time from winter to spring, the time taken for the tree to grow leaves—Lucky has grown dumb. "Since when?" enquires Vladimir; and the whole of Beckett's anguish at the condition of man-in-time bursts forth in Pozzo's reply:

Have you not done tormenting me with your accursed time? It's abominable. When! When! One day, is that not enough for you, one day like any other day, one day he went dumb, one day I went blind, one day we'll go deaf, one day we were born, one day we'll die, the same day, the same second, is that not enough for you?[3]

In spite of his involvement with Didi and Gogo, it is interesting to note that Pozzo's plunge towards timelessness is not identical with theirs. They are headed for infinite duration; he is caught up in a rush towards instantaneity—two aspects of the identical phenomenon but none the less different in their effects.[4] Meanwhile, however, there are other complications. To begin with, time has to be passed ("killed," Malone would say) while waiting—Vladimir and Estragon invent themselves innumerable little "games," usually with words, for, like The Unnamable, they *are* the words they speak, they have no other accessible reality. "That's right," says Vladimir, "let's contradict each other," or else "let's abuse each other"; and at the end, "that wasn't such a bad little canter," says Estragon, or else "how time flies when one has fun!"

The "killing" of time, however, is a chancy business; for it soon becomes clear that the nearer they approach to an escape from temporality, the greater the danger of merely exchanging time as an infinite continuum for time as a series of cycles. Vladimir's song, which opens Act II, already holds a hint of the danger: but Beckett never allows us to forget that his "characters" are also actors (clowns in a circus-ring), and that, as such, they will be back again tomorrow night, or at the next revival, repeating their actions exactly as before. "It's awful," says Vladimir, "It's worse that being at the theatre / The circus / The music-hall / The circus." This exchange, besides exemplifying the circular form of dialogue which is so characteristic of the play, also brings in yet another element—the audience, with its own time-rhythms, its ability to "compel" Vladimir and Estragon "to be back tomorrow," its God-like power to give the characters a "reality" by "witnessing" them. Between the two acts, there is a small, an infinitely small progression: some time has passed. But between tonight and tomorrow night, the cycle of time will have revolved, and all is to be begun again.

Waiting for Godot, then, is the *angoisse* of man at grips with time, the finite clutching at the infinite. But Beckett's genius in the play lies in weaving the inconclusiveness of his rational system into a pattern of imagery so complex, that almost every line suggests another train of images and ideas leading, like the extremities of parabolas, towards infinity. *Nothing* ends: neither the "story of the Englishman in a brothel," nor the argument about the Two Thieves; or if it does, for practical dramatic purposes, the termination is utterly arbitrary and inconclusive, like Lucky's speech. Even Beckett's puns suggest a kind of infinity: when Estragon tries to drown himself, it is (in the French version) "dans la Durance." One by one, the ever-recurrent themes and symbols of Beckett's thought make their appearance—the "closed system," the "horizontal man" ("ce qu'on est bien parterre," says the French Estragon, after the general collapse in Act II), the failure of communication, the search for the Self, the *Néant*, the Others, the tyranny of words, etc., etc.: but each in the form of a suggestion, an allusion, left hanging in the air for the spectator to make what he can of. And the most tantalising of these elusive hints, these inconclusive invitations to a journey without an end, is Godot.

Godot. Godeau, the veteran French racing-cyclist, the "man-on-a-bicycle."[5] Fr.: *godillot*, "a hob-nailed boot." Russ.: *god*, "a year"—old Father Time himself. Or Charl-*ot*, Pierr-*ot*, God-*ot*. Just clowns. Comic grotesques, incarnations of impotence . . . like God? One may speculate till the cows come home, the only certain answer is that there is no answer. Godot is the name which indicates that which cannot be defined, conceived even . . . which some call God, others simply Nothing. Perhaps the two are synonymous, anyway. The fact remains, however, that if Beckett is very far from being a Christian, he is equally far from being an atheist in any blunt materialistic sense. His people, without exception, are haunted and tortured by the idea of God. Do what they will, they cannot escape it:

> ESTRAGON: Do you think God sees me?
> VLADIMIR: You must close your eyes.
> ESTRAGON: God have pity on me!
> VLADIMIR: And me?
> ESTRAGON: On me! On me! Pity! On me![6]

Godot is full of Biblical allusions (the Two Thieves, Cain and Abel, Christ going barefoot, the "Marché du Saint-Sauveur"), but no more so than the other works. Murphy's "mew in West Brompton" becomes in French "l'Impasse de l'Enfant Jésus." *All That Fall* and *More Pricks than Kicks* hark back, one to the Old Testament, the other to the New. Not one of Beckett's people is able to accept either a religious or an atheistical position.

Asked if they believe in God, they reply somewhat hesitantly "no,"[7] and then either curse him for not existing ("The bastard! He doesn't exist!"[8]), or alternatively curse him for the misery which he has fastened upon man. For the traditional faith in "a personal God quaquaquaqua with white beard" they seem at first to have nothing but contempt; yet on the other hand, they are spell-bound by the baroque convolutions of theological speculation. Murphy is a sometime theological student; and the doomed frustration of scholastic reason struggling to construct water-tight systems out of wholly unverifiable first-principles has much in common with Beckett's own dialectic of incommensurables. Yet this only touches the surface of the problem.

To say that "God does not exist" (in Beckett's terms) asserts nothing either way about the existence of God. For if "that which exists" is finite, then God, infinite, is precisely "that which does not exist." Nirvana is "that which does not exist"—it is the liberation of the finite by the infinite. "God," wrote Jarry, in the concluding lines of *Dr Faustroll*, "is the tangential point of zero and the infinite"—an excellent definition of Godot. To proceed from this to the suggestion that the only means of communication between the Zero and the Infinite is "words" (cp. *Comment c'est*) is the sort of speculation that only Beckett would dare indulge in, and even he cancels it all out later: "une oreille qui m'écoute de la foutaise OUI."[9] Yet the idea is already implicit in *Godot*. Godot "sends word" by the Boy to Didi and Gogo that he is not coming. *Credo quia impossibile est*: an excellent doctrine for the mystic who believes in a power above reason. But Beckett, accepting *no* power outside reason, holds by the same doctrine, and the outcome is an irreducible contradiction: God is that Being whose non-existence is the only conceivable evidence of his existence. God is the Sartrian *pour-soi*, for whom there exists no Other. Likewise Godot. But of course it is simpler to believe in the Authorised

Version, particularly as (who knows?) there may even be
a correspondence somewhere. It is at least a possibility
(almost anything is a possibility by this stage), even
though the evidence one way or the other is inconclusive.
"One of the Thieves was saved," notes Vladimir, and
then adds optimistically, "It's a reasonable percentage."

Considered as an expression of Beckett's philosophy of
the inconclusive, *Waiting for Godot* is well-nigh perfect;
considered as drama, it tends to be slightly two-dimen-
sional in conception. By contrast, *Fin de partie* (1956) is
one of the most brilliantly coherent and consistent one-act
plays in the repertory of the drama. We are back in
Malone's world again, the room which is a closed system,
with its two windows like eyes, looking out on all that
remains of an irrelevant world. In the centre of the room
dwells Hamm, the Self, blind and motionless, not even a
reality, but an actor acting the Self—scarcely that, perhaps, rather a stage-prop, from which, as from the seats
in the stalls, the dustsheets are removed before the performance and replaced as soon as it is over. About him
revolves his servant (perhaps also his son), Clov—the
"I" detached from the Self, having no reality save as a
"vice-exister" of the Self, just as the Self is a Nothing, a
void, without the "I"; both eternally incompatible with
each other, and yet eternally inseparable:

> HAMM: I can't leave you.
> CLOV: I know. And you can't follow me.[10]

Behind the present lies the past. Behind Hamm, each
ensconced in a dustbin, legless, like Mahood in his jar,
live Nagg and Nell, Hamm's parents—unforgivable and
arbitrary authors of that beginning which has no end.
Perhaps the locality is no longer Purgatory, but simply
Hell—there are suggestions of it in the alternations of
heat and cold, a foretaste of that "burning sun" which
later tortures the existence of Winnie—but if so, it is Hell
by virtue of its very proximity to Paradise. Even more

than Estragon, Hamm is on the very brink of timelessness: the end is *there*, within reach, and yet, like Zeno's heap, as far removed as ever from realisation:

> Moment upon moment, pattering down, like the millet grains of . . . that old Greek, and all life long you wait for that to mount up to a life.[11]

All this is very familiar—the impotence, the clowning, the themes of the impossibility of birth and death, of ending and beginning, the "games" and the unfinished stories invented to "pass the time." What is new (apart from the condensation of the material, which is un-equalled elsewhere) is the fact that the play itself has become "a game"—to be precise, a game of chess, with Hamm as the King, helpless, his moves confined (in his chair on castors) to one square in any direction, Nagg and Nell as pawns, Clov as the Knight:

> CLOV: When there were still bicycles, I wept to have one. I crawled at your feet. You told me to get out to hell. Now there are none.
> HAMM: And your rounds? When you inspected my paupers. Always on foot?
> CLOV: Sometimes on horse. . . .[12]

"Me to play," murmurs Hamm repeatedly, and at the end, "Old endgame lost of old, play and lose and have done with losing." But this, of course, is precisely what he cannot do. The end is not check-mate, but rather stale-mate, as inevitably it must be against an opponent as elusive as Time . . . or Mr Endon. As the curtain falls, Clov is about to go—but doesn't. Nell seems to be dead, but there is no real evidence. All, in fact, is as it was be-fore. One millionth part of a grain has been added to the heap, and the heap is still unfinished.

By contrast, however, to the lingering and resistant immortality of the Self, the world outside seems to be moving rapidly towards its conclusion. The view which

Clov has through the windows is one of utter desolation. Outside the cell, the "refuge" which is the Self, time has continued and, in its expected fashion, destroyed. This bleak vision of destruction is recurrent in Beckett's thought. "I once knew a madman," says Hamm:

> who thought the end of the world had come. He was a painter—and engraver. I had a great fondness for him. I used to go and see him, in the asylum. I'd take him by the hand and drag him to the window. Look! There! All that rising corn! And there! Look! The sails of the herring-fleet! All that loveliness! He'd snatch away his hand and go back into his corner. Appalled. All he had seen was ashes. He alone had been spared. . . .[13]

Inevitably—the scientists have proved it to us—the world will end, the universe will end, and time will cancel out the minutest vestiges of our significance. And we (our Selves), immortal, timeless, are a "game" to pass the time—a "game" as ultimately meaningless as chess. And God does not exist. Three steps along the road to Nothingness. But the void of *Endgame* is no longer Murphy's old Nirvana, but rather Arsène's dark abyss: the terrifying farcicality of the Absurd. There is a ring of despair about *Endgame* which seems to suggest a crisis in Beckett's thought. Hitherto his art had grappled with the inconceivable and found in it a kind of meaning. Now, suddenly, the very concept of "meaning" seems abhorrent to him—it is the last illusion, the one remaining unreality which can still impose its falsehood upon his relentless awareness:

> HAMM: Clov!
> CLOV: What is it?
> HAMM: We're not beginning to . . . to . . . mean something?
> CLOV: Mean something! You and I, mean something! Ah that's a good one![14]

Endgame is shot through with a ferocious bitterness which has not hitherto appeared in Beckett's work—a bitterness directed against all that lives, since, while there is life, the illusion of meaning may subsist. All that is living must be killed, exterminated without pity—the flea that Clov discovers, the rat in the kitchen, the strange "child" outside. Hamm is utterly ruthless, it is his primary characteristic. He is without mercy and without love; and such involuntary elements of "sympathy" as remain to him, he fritters away deliberately on the toy dog Clov has made for him. His ruthlessness, however, implies no moral judgment against him (there are no moral judgments in Beckett); it is a stage in a dialectic—the basic dialectic of the Absurd. It is quite obvious to thinkers such as Sartre, Camus, Genet or Ionesco that the traditional categories of "meaning"—civilisation, history, religion, ethics, social progress, beauty, art, individual self-realisation—are valueless illusions. And yet the human mind cannot divest itself entirely of all belief in its own significance. There *must* be a meaning somewhere. But if that meaning is ever to be discovered, it can only be by way of a total lucidity. First dispel the illusions of significance, and then it is just conceivable that, out of a totality of unmeaning, a new and hitherto unsuspected awareness of meaning may arise. The method is classic: it is Descartes' process of universal doubt applied now, not simply to the problem of knowledge, but to the human condition as a whole. And *Endgame* follows the logic of this dialectic about as far as it can go, within the terms of rationality. The terrifying power of the play, however, springs from the fact that Beckett himself seems to lose sight of the role of "despair" as a functional element in an Existentialist dialectic. It is as though he himself must first actually experience this despair, and drain the very dregs of his own impotence and purposeless futility, before he can proceed further. *Endgame* is full of phrases whose hopelessness has rarely been equalled: "Nothing is funnier than unhappiness . . ." or, "Use your head, can't you, use your head, you're on earth, there's no cure for that."

And yet, in the strange ending to the play (inexplicably abbreviated in the English version), it is as though, out of the very desolation of un-meaning, a hint of meaning had suddenly emerged. Clov looks through the window and sees a child, whose attitudes seem to suggest at the same time Moses, and Christ resurrected, and the Buddha. Immediately Hamm adds a new degree of despair—that of his own essential Self—to the other which already embraced the totality. "It's the end, Clov, we've come to the end, I don't need you any more." Not that, for one instant, Hamm sees a "meaning" for himself in the symbolic figure. On the contrary, for the dialectic of the Absurd decrees that the very concept of meaning, in any non-illusory sense, can arise only out of a total lucidity, out of an unremitting and all-pervasive awareness of un-meaning . . . which is the situation as the curtain falls. Hamm, meaningless in time, imprisoned in a meaningless universe and impotent to escape from it, incapable of dying, futility eked out with the dimensions of the eternal, is covered with his dustsheet, his Saint-Veronica handkerchief spread over his face, and left in the darkened theatre, only to be resurrected in another cycle of time when next the curtain rises.

Any suspicions of orthodox "religious feeling" which may have been engendered by *Waiting for Godot* or by the final scene of *Endgame* are rudely dispelled by *All That Fall*. *All That Fall* (1956) is Beckett's first play written specifically for radio, and at first hearing, its inner purpose is all but lost in a smoke-screen of Irish burlesque, satire and apparent "realism." If *Endgame* is the most abstract and metaphysical of Beckett's dramas, *All That Fall* is the most "naturalistic"—in fact it contains more characterisation, more conventional psychology and more local colour than anything else that Beckett has written. But this "realism" soon reveals some very significant inconsistencies. Old Maddy Rooney, as she sets off on her painful walk to the station to meet her blind husband, Dan, is nothing but a decrepit and grotesque old hag, a sort of female Molloy; by the time she returns, guiding Dan homeward to their cottage, she has developed into a blue-stocking taking notes on lectures and hoping that one day psycho-analysis may "shed a little light on my lifelong preoccupation with horses' buttocks." Nor is there any more inherent probability in the fact that Dan, a dreary and cantankerous old miser, should glibly quote Dante and refer to Grimm's Law with familiarity.

The realism of *All That Fall*, in fact, is no more than an outward show; it has no intrinsic value of its own. It is Beckett putting into practice his own conviction, that the human pseudo-Self is literally "made of other peoples' words"—and the radio-play is the severest test of the truth of this belief. Without the help of narrative, with no visual aid, with nothing but mere words, Beckett sets out to prove that he can "create" the physical reality of old Maddy and blind Dan, of Christy and Mr Tyler and Miss Fitt, of Foxrock station and the Leopardstown racecourse. And he succeeds. The experiment confirms the hypothesis—but with this twist, that Maddy herself is not merely made of alien words, but is actually aware of it herself. Every now and then, the word-maker deliberately makes her wrong; he uses the wrong word for her, and consequently she *is* wrong:

> Do you not find anything . . . bizarre about my way of speaking? I do not mean the voice. No, I mean the words. I use none but the simplest words, I hope, and yet sometimes I find my way of speaking very . . . bizarre.[15]

The "realism" of the play, in fact, is not a reality. The reality of *All That Fall* lies in its obsession; its theme harks right back to "Dante and the Lobster"—the obsessive theme of death, no longer the *angoisse* of the Self that cannot die, but the arbitrary and intolerable fact of death itself. And it is this fact of death (the ultimate Absurd) which, for Beckett's people, implies a relentless indictment, an unremitting hatred of that "God" of whom the preacher speaks. From the opening strains of *Death and the Maiden* to the final revelation that the reason why the train was late was that a child had been crushed to death beneath the wheels (the question of Dan's guilt hangs over all the play like a threat, but is never answered)— the whole drama is a litany of death. Maddy's daughter, Minnie, and Mr Slocum's mother, and Christy's wife, and the leaves in the ditch, and Mr Slocum's car ("All this morning she went like a dream, and now she is dead . . ."), and the hen on the road:

> MRS ROONEY: Mind the hen! [*Scream of brakes. Squawk of hen*] Oh, mother, you have squashed her, drive on, drive on! . . . What a death! One minute picking happy at the dung, on the road, in the sun, with now and then a dust bath, and then—bang! —all her troubles over. All the laying and the hatching. Just one great squawk and then . . . peace.[16]

Within this context, the title of the play, with all that it implies, is revealed as a sinister and mocking irony:

> MR ROONEY: Who is the preacher tomorrow? [. . .] Has he announced his text?
> MRS ROONEY: "The Lord upholdeth all that fall and raiseth up all those that be bowed down."[17]

—yet the child fell out of the train, and the Lord upheld her not. After Maddy has spoken the text, she and Dan "join in wild laughter." This is a far cry from Estragon's comparing himself to Christ. The essential Self, Beckett seems to be saying, may be timeless: but the "I," the self

I know, is condemned to death, to unbelievable suffering; and this gratuitous misery and futility can only have been ordained by the cruel whim of a "God" who is himself of the same element—words—and understands what he is inflicting. Indeed, the very act of naming "God," as the preacher does, let alone of defining him, conceiving his attributes, is to create an illusion and to engender an evil falsehood. A "God" who is conceivable is a monstrous and malevolent projection of the Other. If there *is* a total reality, an eternal *pour-soi*, it is the absolute Unnamable; as soon as the Preacher calls on "God," all he does is to create a corresponding *en-soi* (the Void's own pseudo-Self, or vice-exister), concocted out of human words and reflecting human evil. The Preacher's "God" is the God of death, destruction and torture. He upholdeth no-one. Only the wordless Self, and not the Preacher, may perhaps go beyond death to the very brink of another reality.

It is possible that *All That Fall* may have been deliberately conceived as a corrective to some of the more misguided interpretations of *Waiting for Godot*; in any case, although successful, it is a comparatively minor work. Beckett's other play for radio, *Embers* (1959), is not only minor, but one of his very few failures. It is technically interesting, and some of its final passages foreshadow the style of *Comment c'est*. But its middle sections hover uneasily between the banal and the melodramatic, and in the end it leaves little more than an unstatisfactory feeling of obscurity never properly resolved. By contrast, *Krapp's Last Tape*, written in 1958 for the legitimate stage, resolves a host of problems which might have seemed well-nigh insoluble.

The central theme of Beckett's philosophy—the impenetrable tangle of relationships between the essential Self and the apparent Self—drove him necessarily in the novel towards the form of the extended monologue. On turning to the theatre, he abandoned this, for obvious reasons: and *Godot, Endgame*, and *All That Fall* use a form of dialogue which, for all its originality of treatment, is fundamentally traditional. But the compulsive forces which demanded the monologue have not ceased to operate, and *Krapp's Last Tape* is Beckett's first experiment in designing for the stage a monologue which is at the same time, in the full sense of the word, dramatic. Krapp is still Belacqua—an aged, sordid, clownish and very decrepit Belacqua, but condemned as always to live again in the dream-reality of the instantaneous present, his past existence. But this is the age of science, and Krapp possesses one gadget which was absent in Ante-Purgatory: a tape-recorder. As he lived, he recorded his life, himself, at intervals on tape. His past is, in a more literal sense than ever before, words: not the misleading words of memory, confused, or partially confused, with images, but words which are pure sound and nothing else— words, too, which telescope all time into a continuous present, for Krapp *is* the voice of Krapp; yet the Krapp on the stage is the future to the voice of Krapp on the tape. The voice of Krapp embodies a whole series of degrees of pastness, and yet exists only in the present: switch off the apparatus, and there is no sound—Nothing. The machine itself is Krapp's identity—an identity which Krapp's Self contemplates with horror and disgust: "Hard to believe I was ever that young whelp. The voice! Jesus! And the aspirations!"[18]

But the machine, too, is caught up in time, in the cycles of eternity. Even when silent, Krapp's life in time is still *there*, on the spools: press the button, and it all begins again, identical. "Here I end," speaks the voice of Krapp; promptly, Krapp switches off, winds the tape back and switches on again. Once more, there is no end. Only if the tape itself contained nothing but silence could there be an end of speaking. But to say: "Here I end" is not to end, for now the words exist, potentially repeatable *ad infinitum*. Each word is a Sartrian act, engendered out of nothing, but once engendered, possessed of an indestructible existence. *Krapp's Last Tape* makes tangible and visible, in its forty minutes between curtain-rise and curtain-fall, the whole *impasse* of Existentialism.

There is, however, another theme in Krapp, emerging to the surface again after years of underground existence, and that is the theme of love. It may seem paradoxical to suggest, in view of the almost legendary sordidness and impotence with which Beckett invests his lovers (most typically, Macmann and Moll) that love is in fact one of the most persistent ideals in Beckett's writings. But there is an analogy with Beckett's people in their search for God. Just as the majority of his characters revile the God that they can conceive, as a malevolent and impotent impostor, yet by their very imprecations hint at the existence of an Absolute beyond conception, so do they also revile the love they know, and by so doing, hint at the same time at the existence of a love which they have never known and cannot know—the love which is "music, *music*, MUSIC." If Beckett's people turn away from love, it is in an agony of disappointed idealism. Love seems to promise a *Nirvana à deux*, an annihilation of time, and has failed to fulfil its promise. Everything is against it. The beloved is the enemy, the Other; lover and beloved are executioner and victim; love is the arbitrary engendering of life in time—the unforgivable act. And yet, obstinately, in Beckett's later work, the ideal re-appears—and once again accompanied by music. It is a music which has lost its Vinteuil-romanticism, has degenerated into the toneless chanting or humming of vulgar ditties; and the love-ideal, similarly, has grown so tentative that it is scarcely recognisable—yet it is there all the same: the tenderness of Vladimir for Estragon, the "bons moments," in spite of all, that Bom spent with Pim; Maddy's grotesque longing for love:

Love, that is all I asked, a little love, daily, twice daily, fifty years of twice daily love like a Paris horse-butcher's regular, what normal woman wants affection?[19]

—and now Krapp. Krapp, if he fails to find the "end" that all Beckett's people are searching for, none the less finds a strange quietus—not a happiness, but a sort of stilling of movement, a slowing down of time, a hesitation on the brink of oblivion:

I asked her to look at me and after a few moments ... after a few moments she did. [...] We drifted in among the flags and stuck. The way they went down, sighing, before the stem! ... I lay down across her with my face in her breasts and my hand on her. We lay there without moving. But under us all moved, and moved us, gently, up and down, and from side to side.[20]

Three times Krapp sets the machine of his identity back to this same point, lulled by its slow, narcotic rhythms. For the first time since *Murphy* we get a glimpse of women who are not hags. "The face she had, the eyes! Like ... chrysolite! ... Ah well." Here, for the first time, is an experience of sex which is not the furthest point of degradation. Not that there is any conclusion: love, like the Self, knows no escape from time. But the memory of this ephemeral, irrational tenderness remains, despite its evident futility, and in fact it suffuses the whole background of *Happy Days*, where, again for the first time, the central figure is a woman.

Winnie, from her opening prayer to her closing love-ditty, occupies the centre of the stage, "stuck up to her diddies in the bleeding ground"—or rather, in the Zeno-heap of days. For her, as for Hamm and Clov, Vladimir and Estragon, time has staggered almost to a standstill, only to leave her entangled in eternal cycles of recurrences. The units of time have grown meaningless, yet she cannot resist them; they have a sort of "old-world

H

flavour" about them, which contributes to her happiness, and she treasures them nostalgically, much as other women would treasure the decorations off a wedding-cake. In fact, she has a special smile reserved for them, as when she reads the instructions on her medicine-bottle:

> six level . . . tablespoonsfuls daily—[*head up, smile*]—the old style!—[*smile off, head down, reads*]—daily . . . before and after . . . meals. . . .[21]

Didi and Gogo still hoped for night to come—not so Winnie. For her, the daylight is endless, it needs a bell to tell her when it is "time" to wake and when it is "time" to sleep. She is dead already, perhaps: this may be Hell ("this hellish sun . . ." "this blaze of hellish light . . ."); if so, then Hell is what lies between death and the end of time.

However, Winnie's strangest characteristic is her "happiness"—a happiness which is almost more frightening that the despair of *Endgame*. "Did you ever have an instant of happiness?" asked Hamm, and Clov replied, "Not to my knowledge."[22] Hamm and Clov are still aware of their own *angoisse*; there may be no end to suffering, but at least they know they suffer. But Winnie is *resigned*: she is the incarnation of the Proustian concept of "habit" which dulls suffering, of which Beckett once wrote: "and the idea that [. . .] suffering will cease is more unbearable than that suffering itself."[23] Winnie has crossed the bar. Not for her the unremitting lucidity of those abdicated intellectuals, Molloy, Malone or Krapp. Winnie is the plebs, the ad-mass, eager to devour any old untruth, to make use of any "pillow of old words" for her head, provided that it keeps her happy. She will believe that black is white, if such a belief is comforting. She will even believe that God is good, that Hell is Heaven as the Preacher promised. "Another heavenly day," her monologue begins, and her speech is studded with fragments of hymns and scraps of prayers:

no no—mustn't complain—so much to be thankful for
—no pain—hardly any—wonderful thing that—
[...] occasional mild migraine—it comes—then goes
—ah yes—many mercies—prayers perhaps not for
naught—first thing—last thing. . . .[24]

There is irony in this, of course, and a great deal of
bitterness: but there is also much pity. Winnie is a victim,
a victim of the human condition; and if her only defence
against the impossible and the intolerable is to behave
and feel as though it were all "natural" and "very understandable—most understandable," who is there to blame
her? She has, of course, the usual consolations of existence
—she tells herself "stories," she has her "bag," her hoard
of miscellaneous possessions, like Malone—her subconscious, her memories, her fruitless temptations of
suicide. She exercises her intellect by reading the words
on the handle of her toothbrush and learning the meaning
of the term "hog"; she has even the futile consolations of
her sexuality—her lipstick, her ornate hat, her bosom,
her nail-file—but her most formidable weapon of defence
against the Absurd is her indifference. Whatever is, is
right—and she is "happy."

In terms of the Proustian attitude to suffering—an
attitude which, in the *Trilogy*, was essentially that of
Beckett also—*Happy Days* is the most pessimistic play
that Beckett has written, and perhaps this is the intention.
It is as though the ultimate *Néant* had been preceded by a
false *Néant*, in which time had simply run down rather
than stopped, had disintegrated accidentally, without
thereby resolving all past and future into an instantaneous
present. Winnie's monologue is almost as full of negatives
as *Watt*, but they are the small, mean negatives of practical life ("no more medicine," "no more toothpaste"),
they seem to have lost their symbolic function, to refer
simply to medicine and toothpaste and not, by implication, as they still did in *Endgame* ("no more bicycles . . .

no more coffins . . . no more painkiller") to an ultimate which cannot be defined except by negation. Winnie's days are empty, utterly empty—yet they still retain their attributes as *days*:

> Ah yes, so little to say, so little to do, and the fear so great, certain days, of finding oneself . . . left, with hours still to run, before the bell for sleep, and nothing more to say, nothing more to do, that the days go by, certain days go by, quite by, the bell goes, and little or nothing said, little or nothing done.[25]

For Estragon, sleep was intolerable, for to sleep was to lose identity, to cease to exist. But Winnie couldn't care less—nor Willie either, for that matter. To Willie, it is a matter of supreme indifference whether he is alive or dead, existing or not existing. He has given up. And so he sleeps. Sleep is as good a means as any other to pass a time which will not let itself be passed.

Yet in spite of all this, Winnie has her Willie. Not that Willie is the ideal hero, or even the ideal husband. He is as decrepit as Molloy, although rather better dressed: "Not the crawler you were, poor darling. No, not the crawler I gave my heart to."[26] He snoozes, he reads the paper. He prefers his pornographic postcards to the sexual reality of Winnie. He keeps his back turned to her, scarcely replies to her questions and then only in monosyllables. After fifteen minutes, Willie utters his first word: "It." "Oh you are going to talk to me today," exclaims Winnie, "this is going to be a happy day! Another happy day." The ideal, suggested in *Krapp's Last Tape*, of a communication achieved through love which escapes the falsehood of words, fails completely. All through the play, Winnie addresses herself to Willie, longs for him to come to her; yet she is not even sure that there was ever "love" between them; and when at last he does appear before her, perhaps even desiring her again, she turns on him with all the vulgar sarcasms of a nagging harridan:

> Well this is an unexpected pleasure! Reminds me of the day you came whining for my hand. I worship you, Winnie, be mine. Life a mockery without Win. What a get up, you do look a sight![27]

Strangely, however, although the manifestations of their "love" are about as discouraging as they could be, this relationship seems none the less to be the only reality in Winnie's empty world. The words of her little song ("Though I say not / What I may not / Let you hear, / Yet the swaying / Dance is saying / Love me dear!"), inane as they are, seem to embody the essence of a relationship which does in fact exist, even though it is unattainable in practice, perhaps even inexpressible in any terms. Certainly Winnie *needs* Willie—but her need seems to be based on a rational argument, unusually baroque even for Beckett, rather than an emotion. Her "proof" of the existence of love is a simplified version of that which the "I" of *Comment c'est* uses to demonstrate the necessity for the existence of God. Winnie's "Self" is words, and the word is a means of communication—therefore the spoken word presupposes a listener: a word spoken without a listener to communicate with would be absurd. Winnie (like Molloy) speaks all the time, therefore Willie *must* be there to listen:

> Ergo you are there. Oh no doubt you are dead, like the others, no doubt you have died, or gone away and left me, like the others, it doesn't matter, you are there.[28]

But only the lover (or God) will be there *all* the time to listen to his beloved, *ergo* there must be such a thing as love.

How seriously Beckett intends us to take this Gilbertian bit of reasoning is not clear. Indeed, there are several aspects, both of *Comment c'est* and *Happy Days* which are unclear, and will probably remain so until Beckett himself elucidates them. None the less, Winnie's attitude corresponds well enough to the Beckettian analysis of love. For if the essential Self is a void, what communication can there be between two such voids that can be demonstrated, save by a pretty baroque sort of Logic? And yet, if there *were* a reality of love, a love which could pierce the pseudo-Self of personality, then the whole situation of the Self in relation to the Totality might be altered. Not that we should expect from Beckett any sudden revelation. If love exists, it is, like God, in spite of, not because of, the evidence. By all the evidence, it is plainly impossible; yet Beckett's art is precisely that of the impossible, and this art has not yet reached its end.

REFERENCES

1. *W.F.G.*, p. 34.
2. *E.*, p. 12.
3. *W.F.G.*, p. 89.
4. See Ross Chambers, "Beckett's Brinkmanship," 1963, pp. 57–75.
5. Beckett himself gave this "clue" (?) to Prof. Kenner.
6. *W.F.G.*, pp. 76–7.
7. *E.g.*, *C.C.*, pp. 91 and 119.
8. *E.*, p. 38.
9. *C.C.*, p. 175.
10. *E.*, p. 33.
11. *E.*, p. 45.
12. *E.*, p. 15.
13. *E.*, p. 32.
14. *E.*, p. 27.
15. *All That Fall*, p. 8.
16. *Op. cit.*, pp. 14–15.
17. *Op. cit.*, pp. 35–6.
18. *K.L.T.*, p. 18.
19. *All That Fall*, p. 9.
20. *K.L.T.*, p. 18.
21. *H.D.*, p. 13.
22. *E.*, p. 42.
23. *Proust*, p. 42.
24. *H.D.*, pp. 11–12.
25. *H.D.*, p. 27.
26. *H.D.*, pp. 34–5.
27. *H.D.*, p. 45.
28. *H.D.*, p. 38.

BIBLIOGRAPHY

All editions cited in the text or references are marked *****. *The translations (into French or English) are by Beckett himself unless otherwise stated. S.B. = Samuel Beckett.*

I. SAMUEL BECKETT

A. Works originally written in English.

1. Verse

Whoroscope. Paris (The Hours Press) 1930. Reprinted in ******Poems in English*.

Echo's Bones and Other Precipitates. Paris (Europa Press) 1935. Reprinted in ******Poems in English*, also in *Gedichte* (1959) and *Evergreen Review*, No. 1 (1957).

Poems in English. *****London (Calder) 1961. New York (Grove Press) 1962.

2. Novels and Stories

More Pricks than Kicks. *****London (Chatto & Windus) 1934. One story from this collection, "Dante and the Lobster," reprinted in *Evergreen Review*, No. 1 (1957).

Murphy. London (Routledge) 1938. Reprinted, Paris (Olympia Press) and New York (*****Grove Press) 1958; London (Calder) in preparation. French translation: Paris (Bordas) 1947; (Minuit) 1953.

Watt (written 1942–4). Paris (Olympia) 1953, 2nd edn., *****1958. Reprinted, New York (Grove Press) 1959; London (Calder) 1961.

From an Abandoned Work. (B.B.C. Third Programme, 14 Dec. 1957.) *Evergreen Review*, No. 3 (1957); London (*****Faber) 1958.

3. Plays for Stage and Radio

All That Fall. (B.B.C. Third Programme, 13 Jan. 1957.) London (*****Faber) 1957; New York (Grove Press) 1960. French translation, by Robert Pinget: *Tous ceux qui tombent*. Paris (Minuit) 1957.

Krapp's Last Tape. (Royal Court Theatre, 28 Oct. 1958.) *Evergreen Review*, No. 5 (1958). London (*****Faber) 1959; New York (Grove Press) 1960. French translation: *La Dernière Bande*. Paris (Minuit) 1959.

Embers. (B.B.C. Third Programme, 24 Jun. 1959). London (*****Faber) 1959; *Evergreen Review*, No. 10, Nov.–Dec. 1959, pp. 28–41; New York (Grove Press) 1960. French translation, by S.B. and Robert Pinget: *Cendres*. Paris (Minuit) 1959.

Act Without Words II. New York (*Grove Press) 1960.

Happy Days. (Cherry Lane Theatre, New York, 17 Sep. 1961.) New York (Grove Press) 1961; London (*Faber) 1962. French translation: *Oh les beaux jours.* Paris (Minuit) 1963.

Words and Music (play for radio). *Evergreen Review,* No. 27, Nov.–Dec. 1962, pp. 34–43.

4. Criticism

"Dante . . . Bruno. Vico . . . Joyce," in *Our Exagmination round his Factification for Incamination of Work in Progress.* Paris (Shakespeare & Co.) 1929; reprinted, London (*Faber) 1961, pp. 1–22.

Proust. London (Chatto & Windus) 1931. Reprinted, New York (*Grove Press) 1957.

"Three Dialogues" (by S.B. and Georges Duthuit, on Tal Coat, Masson and Bram van Velde). In *Transition Forty-Nine,* No. 5, pp. 97–103.

5. Translations into English

Anthology of Mexican Poetry (compiled by Octavio Paz, preface by C. M. Bowra). Indiana University Press, 1958 (Unesco Collection of Representative Works, Latin American Series); London (*Thames & Hudson) 1958.

The Old Tune. (B.B.C. Third Programme, 21 Aug. 1960.) Tr. of *La Manivelle,* by Robert Pinget. Paris (*Minuit) 1960 (bilingual text).

B. Works originally written in French

1. Verse

Poèmes 38–39. In *Temps modernes,* No. 14, Nov. 1946, pp. 288–93. Reprinted in *Gedichte.*

Trois poèmes. In *Transition Forty-Eight* (bilingual text), pp. 96–7. Reprinted in *Poems in English* and in *Gedichte.*

Trois poèmes. In *Cahiers des saisons,* No. 2, Oct. 1955.

Gedichte (contains *Echo's Bones* and two groups of French poems). Wiesbaden (Limes) 1959.

2. Novels and Stories

Mercier et Camier (written c. 1945). Unpublished.

Molloy. Paris (Minuit) 1951. Reprinted, Paris (Union générale d'Éditions) 1963, with useful selection of criticism. Eng. translation by S.B. and Patrick Bowles, Paris (Olympia) 1955. Reprinted in *Three Novels,* *London (Calder) 1959; New York (Grove Press) 1960. A fragment of an earlier version appears in *Transition Fifty,* pp. 103–5.

Malone Meurt. Paris (Minuit) 1951. Eng. translation, *Malone Dies,*

New York, (Grove Press) 1956; London (Calder) 1958, reprinted in *Three Novels*, *1959. Penguin Books, 1962. A fragment of an earlier version appears in *Transition Fifty*, pp. 105–6.

L'Innommable. Paris (Minuit) 1953. Eng. translation, *The Unnamable*, New York (Grove Press) 1958, reprinted in *Three Novels*, 1960; London (Calder), in * *Three Novels*, 1959.

Nouvelles et textes pour rien. *Paris (Minuit) 1955. (Containing "La Fin"; "Le Calmant"; "L'Expulsé"; another story, "Premier amour," remains unpublished). "La Fin," tr. by S.B. and Richard Seaver as "The End," in *Evergreen Review*, No. 15, 1960, pp. 22–41. "Text For Nothing I," in *Evergreen Review*, No. 9, 1959. "The Expelled," in *Evergreen Review*, No. 22, Jan.–Feb. 1962, pp. 8–20.

Comment c'est. *Paris (Minuit) 1961. Eng. translation, *How it is*, New York (Grove Press) 1964; London (Calder) in preparation. Extracts in *X*, No. 1, London, 1959, pp. 35–7, and *Evergreen Review*, No. 14, Sep.–Oct. 1960, pp. 58–65, under title "From an Unabandoned Work."

3. Plays and Mimes

Eleuthéria (written *c.* 1947). Unpublished.

En attendant Godot. (Théâtre Babylone, 5 Jan. 1953.) Paris (Minuit) 1952. Eng. translation, *Waiting for Godot*, New York (Grove Press) 1954; London (*Faber) 1956.

Fin de partie. (Royal Court Theatre, London, in French, 3 Apr. 1957.) Paris (Minuit) 1957. Eng. translation, *Endgame*, London (*Faber) 1958; New York (Grove Press) 1958.

Acte sans paroles I. (Mime, music by John Beckett; Royal Court Theatre, 3 Apr. 1957.) Paris (Minuit) 1957. Eng. translation, *Act Without Words* I, London (*Faber) and New York (Grove Press) 1958.

Cascando (for radio). Music by Marcel Mihalovici. Paris (Minuit) 1963 (in preparation). Eng. translation: *Cascando*, in *Evergreen Review*, No. 30, May–Jun. 1963, pp. 47–57.

4. Criticism

Bram Van Velde, by S.B., Georges Duthuit and Jacques Putman. Paris (Musée de Poche) 1958. Edition de luxe (with different text), Torino (Fratelli Pozzo) and Paris (Guy le Prat) 1961. Eng. translation, New York (Grove Press Evergreen Gallery Book) 1960. Contains two articles by S.B., dated 1948 and 1949 respectively; also refers to other comments by S.B. on Bram van Velde in: *Cahiers d'art*, 1945–6; *Derrière le miroir*, Jun. 1948; *Bulletin galerie Michel Warren*, May 1957.

5. Translation into French

Anna Livia Plurabelle (fragment of James Joyce's *Finnegans Wake* translated under Joyce's supervision, *c.* 1930). Published in *Souvenirs de James Joyce*, by Philippe Soupault, Algiers (Charlot) 1943, pp. 73–90.

II. GENERAL CRITICISM (SELECTED)

[Anon]: "Expatriate Writers in Paris," in *Times Literary Supplement*, 27 May 1955.

[Anon]: "Messenger of Gloom: a Profile," in *The Observer*, 9 Nov. 1958.

[Anon]: "Paradise of Indignity," in *Times Literary Supplement*, 28 Mar. 1958, p. 168.

Abel, Lionel: "Joyce the Father, Beckett the Son," in *The New Leader* (N.Y.), 14 Dec. 1959.

Abirached, Robert: "Beckett," in *Ecrivains d'aujourd'hui* (ed. Bernard Pingaud), Paris 1960, pp. 93–100.

Bachmann, Claus-Henning: "Die Hoffnung am Strick," in *Antares* (Mainz), jahrg. VI, No. 3, May 1958, pp. 207–10.

Barbour, Thomas: "Beckett and Ionesco," in *Hudson Review*, Summer 1958, pp. 271–7.

Bataille, Georges: "Le Silence de Molloy," in *Critique*, 15 May, 1951, pp. 387–96.

Blanchot, Maurice: "Où maintenant? Qui maintenant?" in *Le Livre à Venir*, Paris 1959, pp. 256–70. Reprinted in *Evergreen Review*, No. 7 (1959), pp. 222–9.

Brée, Germaine: "Samuel Beckett," in *Configurations Critiques*, Paris 1963.

Brooke-Rose, Christine: "Samuel Beckett and the Anti-Novel," in *London Magazine*, V, No. 12, Dec. 1958, pp. 38–46.

Butler, Michael: "Anatomy of Despair," in *Encore*, May–Jun. 1961, pp. 17–24.

——: *Cahiers de la Compagnie Madeleine Renaud—Jean-Louis Barrault*, Oct. 1963 (special number devoted to S.B.).

Chadwick, C.: "*Waiting for Godot*. A Logical Approach," in *Symposium* XIV, No. 4, Winter 1960, pp. 252–7.

Chambers, Ross: "The Other," in *The Nation* (Sydney), 22 Sep. 1962.

——: "Samuel Beckett and the Padded Cell," in *Meanjin Quarterly* (Melbourne), 1962, No. 4, pp. 451–62.

——: "Beckett's Brinkmanship," in *AUMLA 19* (Christchurch, N.Z.), May 1963, pp. 57–75.

Champigny, Robert: "Interprétation de *En Attendant Godot*," in *P.M.L.A.*, Jun. 1960.

Cmarada, Geraldine: "*Malone Dies*. A Round of Consciousness," in *Symposium*, XIV, No. 3, Fall 1960, pp. 199–212.

CODIGNOLA, LUCIANO: "Il Teatro della Guerra Fredda (III): Samuel Beckett," in *Tempo Presente*, Anno II, No. 1, Jan. 1957, pp. 53–6.

COHN, RUBY: "The Comedy of Samuel Beckett: 'Something old, Something new . . .'," in *Yale French Studies*, No. 23, Summer 1959, pp. 11–17.

——: "Still Novel," in *Yale French Studies*, No. 24, Fall 1959, pp. 48–53.

——: "A Note on Beckett, Dante and Geulincx," in *Comparative Literature*, No. 12, 1960, pp. 93–4. See also under heading *Perspective*.

COE, RICHARD N.: "Le Dieu de Samuel Beckett," in *Cahiers de la Compagnie Madeleine Renaud—Jean-Louis Barrault*, No. 44, Oct. 1963, pp. 6–36.

——: *Samuel Beckett: The Comic Gamut*. Rutgers U. P. 1962.

——: "Samuel Beckett, self-translator," in *P.M.L.A.*, Dec. 1961.

——: "*Watt* in the light of *The Castle*," in *Comparative Literature*, No. 2, Spring 1961.

Collected Criticism of Samuel Beckett. London (Calder) 1963.

CRUICKSHANK, JOHN (ed.): *The Novelist as Philosopher: Studies in French Fiction, 1935–1960*. Oxford 1962: "Beckett," by Martin Esslin, pp. 128–146.

DELYE, HUGUETTE: *Samuel Beckett, ou la philosophie de l'absurde*. Aix-en-Provence (Publications des Annales de la Faculté des Lettres, Série Travaux et Mémoires, No. XVI: *La Pensée Universitaire*) 1960.

EASTMAN, RICHARD: "The Strategy of Samuel Beckett's *Endgame*," in *Modern Drama*, II, No. 1, May 1959, pp. 36–44.

ELLMANN, RICHARD: *James Joyce*. New York and Oxford, 1959.

ESSLIN, MARTIN: *The Theatre of the Absurd*. New York 1961. "Beckett," pp. 1–46. *Bibliography*. See also under CRUICKSHANK, JOHN.

FITCH, BRIAN T.: "Narrateur et narration dans la trilogie romanesque de Samuel Beckett," in *Bulletin des Jeunes Romanistes*, May 1961.

FLOOD, ETHELBERT: "A reading of Beckett's *Godot*," in *Culture*, Sep. 1961.

FOWLIE, WALLACE: "The New French Theater: Artaud, Beckett, Genet, Ionesco," in *Sewanee Review*, LXVII, No. 4, Autumn 1959, pp. 643–57.

FRIEDMAN, MELVIN: "The Novels of Beckett. An Amalgam of Joyce and Proust," in *Comparative Literature*, XII, No. 1, Winter 1960, pp. 47–58.

GESSNER, NIKLAUS: *Die Unzulänglichkeit der Sprache: Eine Untersuchung über Formzerfall und Beziehungslosigkeit bei Samuel Beckett*. Zürich 1957.

GREGORY, HORACE: "Prose and Poetry of Samuel Beckett," in *Commonweal*, LXXI, No. 5, 30 Oct. 1959, pp. 162–3.

GROSSVOGEL, DAVID: *The Self-Conscious Stage in Modern French Drama*. New York 1958. "Beckett," pp. 324–34. *Bibliography*.

GUGGENHEIM, PEGGY: *Confessions of an Art-Addict*. London 1960.

HAMILTON, KENNETH: "Boon or Thorn? Joyce Cary and Samuel Beckett on Human Life," in *Dalhousie Review*, XXXVIII, No. 4, Winter 1959, pp. 433–42.

HANSEN-LÖVE, FRIEDRICH: "Samuel Beckett, oder die Einübung ins Nichts," in *Hochland* (Munich). Jahrg. 50, 1 Heft, Oct. 1957, pp. 36–46.

HARVEY, L. E.: "Art and the Existential in *En Attendant Godot*," in *P.M.L.A.*, No. 75, 1960, pp. 137–46.

HOFFMAN, FREDERICK: *Samuel Beckett, The Language of Self*. In series: *Crosscurrents—Modern Critiques*. Carbondale 1962. *Bibliography*.

HUBERT, RENÉE R.: "The couple and the performance in Samuel Beckett's plays," in *L'Esprit Créateur*, Winter 1962.

ISER, WOLFGANG: "Samuel Becketts dramatische Sprache," in *Germanisch-Romanische Monatsschrift*, Oct. 1961.

KENNER, HUGH: *Samuel Beckett: A Critical Study*. New York 1961; London 1962.

——: "The Beckett Landscape," in *Spectrum*, Winter 1958, pp. 8–24. See also under heading *Perspective*.

——: *Flaubert, Joyce and Beckett: the stoic comedians*. Boston 1962,

KERMODE, FRANK: "Beckett: Snow and Pure Poverty," in *Encounter*, No. 82, Jul. 1960, pp. 73–7.

KERN, EDITH: "Drama stripped for Inaction," in *Yale French Studies*, No. 14, Winter 1954–5, pp. 41–7. See also under heading *Perspective*.

KRAMER-BADONI, RUDOLF: "Die Annihilierung des Nihilismus, ein Versuch über Samuel Beckett," in *Forum* (Vienna), Apr. 1961.

LAMONT, ROSETTE: "The Metaphysical Farce: Beckett and Ionesco," in *French Review*, XXXII, No. 4, Feb. 1959, pp. 319–28.

LEVENTHAL, A. J.: "Close of Play. Reflections on Samuel Beckett's new Work for the French Theatre," in *Dublin Magazine*, Apr.–Jun. 1957, pp. 18–22.

LOY, J. ROBERT: " 'Things' in Recent French Literature," in *P.M.L.A.*, No. 71, 1956, pp. 27–41.

MAILER, NORMAN: "Column Seventeen" and "A Public Notice on *Waiting for Godot*," in *Advertisements for Myself*, London 1961, pp. 262–3 and 266–72.

MARISSEL, ANDRÉ: *Beckett* (*Classiques du XXe Siècle*). Paris (Editions Universitaires) 1963. *Bibliography*.
"L'Univers de Samuel Beckett," in *Esprit*, No. 320, Sep. 1963, pp. 240–55.

MAURIAC, CLAUDE: *L'Alittérature contemporaine*. Paris 1958. Tr. by Samuel I. Stone, *The New Literature*, New York 1959.

PQ 2249
.K4

PC 2001:
.F 75

MAYOUX, JEAN-JACQUES: "Le Théâtre de Beckett," in *Études anglaises*, No. 10, Oct.-Dec. 1957, pp. 350–66. See also under heading *Perspective*.

MIDDLETON, CHRISTOPHER: "Zur Entdeckung neuer Wirklichkeit: Randnotizen zu den Romanen von Samuel Beckett," in *Akzente* (Munich), Jahrg. 4, Heft 5, Oct. 1957, pp. 407–12.

MILLER, KARL: "Beckett's Voices," in *Encounter*, XIII, No. 72, Sep. 1959, pp. 59–61.

MOORE, JOHN: "A Farewell to Something," in *Tulane Drama Review*, v, No. 1, Sep. 1960, pp. 49–60.

NOON, WILLIAM: "Modern Literature and the Sense of Time," in *Thought*, XXXIII, No. 131, Winter 1958–9, pp. 571–603.

NORES, DOMINIQUE: "La Condition humaine selon Beckett," in *Théâtre d'aujourd'hui*, No. 3, Sep.–Oct. 1957, pp. 9–12.

Perspective (Washington University). XI, No. 3, Autumn 1959, special number devoted to Samuel Beckett. Contains: COHN, RUBY: "Preliminary Observations" and *Bibliography*; HOEFER, JACQUELINE: "*Watt*"; KENNER, HUGH: "The Cartesian Centaur"; KERN, EDITH: "Moran-Molloy—The Hero as Author"; MAYOUX, J.-J.: "The Theatre of Samuel Beckett"; and MINTZ, SAMUEL: "Beckett's *Murphy*—A Cartesian Novel."

PINGAUD, BERNARD: "*Molloy*, douze ans après," in *Les Temps Modernes*, Jan. 1963, pp. 1283–1300.

PRONKO, LEONARD: "Beckett, Ionesco, Schehadé: The Avant-Garde Theatre," in *Modern Language Forum*, XLII, 1958, pp. 118–23.

ROBBE-GRILLET, ALAIN: "Samuel Beckett, Auteur dramatique," in *Critique*, Feb. 1953, pp. 108–14.

SCHNEIDER, ALAN: "Waiting for Beckett: A Personal Chronicle," in *Chelsea Review*, No. 2, Autumn 1958, pp. 3–20.

STOTTLAR, JAMES: *Samuel Beckett. An Introduction and an Interpretation*. M.A. Thesis (Columbia University). Unpublished.

STRAUSS, WALTER: "Dante's Belacqua and Beckett's Tramps," in *Comparative Literature*, XI, No. 3, Summer 1959, pp. 250–61.

TINDALL, WILLIAM: "Beckett's Bums," in *Critique*, Spring–Summer 1958, pp. 3–15.

VIGÉE, CLAUDE: "Les Artistes de la Faim," in *Comparative Literature*, IX, No. 2, Spring 1957, pp. 97–117.

III. BIBLIOGRAPHY

1. *Beckett's Works:* There is no complete checklist, but a useful "Chronology" will be found in KENNER, *Samuel Beckett: A Critical Study* (see above, II), pp. 26–7.
2. *Criticism:* Critical articles, etc., on Beckett now number several hundred. There is no complete bibliography. Partial biblio-

graphies will be found in the works listed above, II, under ESSLIN, HOFFMAN, MARISSEL, GROSSVOGEL and *Perspective*. See also:

French VII: Bibliography of Critical and Bibliographical References for the Study of Contemporary French Literature. New York 1956–62.

KLAPP, OTTO: *Bibliographie der Französischen Literaturwissenschaft.* Frankfurt-am-Main, 1960–62.